GREEK ARCHITECTURE

THE GREAT AGES OF WORLD ARCHITECTURE

GREEK   *Robert L. Scranton*
ROMAN   *Frank E. Brown*
EARLY CHRISTIAN AND BYZANTINE   *William L. MacDonald*
MEDIEVAL   *Howard Saalman*
GOTHIC   *Robert Branner*
RENAISSANCE   *Bates Lowry*
BAROQUE AND ROCOCO   *Henry A. Millon*
MODERN   *Vincent Scully, Jr.*
WESTERN ISLAMIC   *John D. Hoag*
PRE-COLUMBIAN   *Donald Robertson*
CHINESE AND INDIAN   *Nelson I. Wu*
JAPANESE   *William Alex*

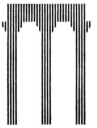

GREEK ARCHITECTURE

by Robert L. Scranton

GEORGE BRAZILLER · NEW YORK

Library of Congress Catalog Card Number: 62-7531

Second Printing, 1965

Illustrations printed in the Netherlands
Text printed in the United States of America

CONTENTS

Text
1. "CLASSIC" GREEK STYLE   9
2. THE FORMS OF NATURE: *Stone Age to Homer:*
   4000–700 B.C.   14
3. THE FORM OF SUBSTANCE: *Homer to Plato:*
   700–400 B.C.   23
4. THE FORM OF KOSMOS: *Plato to Augustus: 400–31 B.C.* 36
5. EPILOGUE: *Augustus to Constantinople:*
   31 B.C.–A.D. 330.   47

Plates   49

Notes   113

Glossary   116

Bibliography   119

Index   122

Sources of Illustrations   127

1 "CLASSIC" GREEK STYLE

The clearest formulation of the characteristic Greek ethos was developed around the middle of the fifth century B.C.; and the monument of this period that best embodies the formulation in architectural terms today is the Hephaisteion in Athens—not the finest of ancient buildings, but standing more nearly in its original form than any other Greek temple (Plates 2–5).

As a temple its primary function was to house the god, or at least, in more worldly, sophisticated terms, to shelter the statue and the possessions of the cult. It is essentially a chamber—a "naos" or "dwelling place"—a "cella." The naos has a porch in front and at the rear. The whole is enclosed within a colonnade supporting a roof, protecting the naos or, perhaps more likely, the visitors seeking escape from rain or sun.

The temple rests on a low foundation, approached from all sides by three steps.[1] The design of the columns combines a supporting shaft with a conical echinus making a transition to the square abacus that actually bears the architrave above. On the architrave rests a frieze whose grooved triglyphs and plain metopes suggest, however inaccurately, the beam construction of the ceiling, while the overhanging cornice above, through the rectangular mutules on its under surface, conveys an idea of the roof structure. Along the edge of the cornice of the building when complete, ran the sima–the gutter–with antefixes at the ends of the rows of cover-tiles on the roof, and outflow spouts between. Along the ridge were ridge-cover-tiles, with special ones bearing palmettes to seal the joints of the regular kind. Standing at the corners and peak of the gable were akroteria–sculptured ornaments.

The chief material of construction was stone; except for the timbering in the ceiling and roof, and the terra-cotta tiles, every-thing was marble cut in large blocks and fastened by means of clamps and dowels. Paint was used to pick out certain moldings and strengthen the contrasting elements of the frieze.

The over-all volume is formed by the peripteron colonnade and ceiling. Within this, in front of the pronaos, is a rectangular volume extending the entire width of the structure, defined by the peripteron columns on three sides and the porch of the pronaos, with the extension of its frieze to the back of the colon-nade, on the other side. Along the sides of the naos run the long, narrow, high volumes of the peripteron colonnade, joining with· that between the façade of the rear porch and the surrounding columns. The volumes of the naos include the pronaos itself, defined by walls on three sides and the two columns "in antis," in front, constituting a recess from the peripteron volume and a passage to the interior. The interior of the naos reverses the exterior of the temple: the inmost space is a colonnade-lined room, surrounded by narrow shallow volumes between the inner colonnade and the walls.

Among the sensory stimuli, that of the sense of movement is partly implied in the approach presented by the steps, and in the awareness of forms lying behind, within the colonnade. It is also in the "rise" of the columns and the sloping roof. More perva-sively it is in the multitude of lines: the physical substance of the steps, the shafts, the architrave, and the other elements; the optical lines defining these shapes–the edges of the steps and so on; the lines of the fluting of the columns and of the details of the entablature above; the lines of the shadows they cast. Still more it is in the rhythms: the succession of columns along the flank and side, alternating with the dark of the intercolumniation, and modulated by the expanding and contracting rhythm of accents of lines of the fluting as they emerge from behind the column on one side and recede on the other; the rhythms of detail in architrave, frieze, and cornice. Not least is it in the play of light, which not only serves to duplicate every line by a shadow, but, as the sun pursues its course, constantly changes the shadows, and keeps them literally in motion.

Light functions, too, in its own right, creating forms of various shapes and intensities of luminosity among the details of the moldings, the flutes of the columns, and the spaces behind the columns. It assumes, indeed, much of the role of color. As black and white, with intermediate values, light constitutes all the color on the lower part of the buildings; in the frieze and above, it plays with the bold flat blues and reds which were characteristic of Greek buildings in bringing out selected elements at this level.

Finally texture: the smoothness of the marble in most parts is modified by the effects of light and line, as in the rippled fluting of the columns, the chunky triglyphs, the floral patterns of the sima.

All these elements are manipulated in the manner of "classic" Hellenism. For example, the forms are "ideal" or "typical"—not particularized or "realistic"—nor, at the other extreme, radically abstracted. All the forms of the Hephaisteion are essentially like the forms of all other Doric buildings. Greek architects did not strive either for marked individuality, or for extreme reduction to theoretical essence. An ancient builder could erect a temple by standard proportions from a relatively brief verbal description specifying only the relatively minor novelties the designer might have occasion to include.[2] Even within the single building, the complete uniformity of repeated elements—such as columns or triglyphs—is abundantly evident.

Another characteristic is the confident objectivity of the rendering. Nothing is offered by illusion, nothing need be projected into the design by the mood or imagination of the observer. Everything is actually present in stone, creating its own direct stimulus to the perceptive faculties of the observer. Nor is the building, or any part of it, symbolic or otherwise meaningful of anything other than what it literally is—a temple, a "naos" for a god, and a protected colonnade for the visitor.

The conspicuous clarity of the design and execution hardly requires elaboration. The carving is sharp and precise, the distinction of elements is uncomplicated and unimpeded. So, too, is the emphasis on mass, on form in three dimensions, on the composition in figures of solid geometry. The forms of mass and volume are simple—rectangular prisms, cylinders, cones—and every device is employed to strengthen the awareness of the whole shape. Thus the columns are not only essentially cylindrical, but the concavity of the flutings calls attention to the body of the stone from which they are cut, and the arrises, or edges between, are literally tangible. The arrises on the receding surfaces of the columns, as they catch increasing concentration of shadow in curving away from the sun, strengthen the visual awareness of the fashioned solid. The shadow of the cornice on the frieze emphasizes the projection and recession of elements of the triglyphs. The proportions of the whole as well of the parts individually are compact, in low ratios avoiding dominance of one dimension over the others.

The actual dynamic developed is one of poise: the building is, as we have seen, live with movement, but always contained within the whole. The predominant verticals and horizontals on the side, and the exact symmetry of the front, might have been completely static, but for the movement; the result is a subtly breathing aliveness at essential rest. Even in the Hephaisteion, though more so in finer buildings, the effect is increased by the more subtle deviations from the vertical and horizontal, chiefly in the inclination of the columns, and the slight curvatures in the columns, steps, and entablature.

The composition is further marked by an even, regular disposition of elements, with a sufficient degree of subordination and dominance to provide a major point of focus on the center of the façade in front and in back, and on a few chosen points within. There are, first, the base, the body, and the crowning elements. The base in turn has three steps; the body has column, intercolumniation, capital; the entablature has architrave, frieze, cornice. The columns in their turn have three elements—shaft, echinus, and abacus; the architrave has the beam itself, the taenia along the top, the regulae beneath this; the frieze has its triglyphs, metopes, and crowning band; the cornice in front forms a triangular pediment, and in itself has its bed molding, mutules, and face. Meanwhile the elements are subdividing also according to a system of twos developed from the columns: a triglyph for each column, and one for each intercolumniation; a mutule on the cornice for each triglyph and one between. These progressions go even further, and constitute a logical development from the solid ground to the minutely articulated roof. The cohesive principle is purely architectonic—the elucidation of the structural nature of each part and its relation to all the others.

Finally, there is complete integration with the environment. From the low horizontal steps, clinging to the ground and repeating the horizontal of the earth, only slightly compressed for the building, the structure rises to the triangular pediment, whose lines broken by akroteria and antefix fit the rectangular building between the flat earth and the domed sky. Moreover the building is equally accessible from every side—the sides and rear as well as the front—and the colonnades, while defining the shape of the building, provide free vision behind them to the naos, free circulation of air and space between the interior and the world around.

In the idealism, objectivity, and literalism; in the clarity, massiveness, and poise; in the regularity, concentration, and architectonic composition; and in the complete integration of the building to its world—in all these elements we may see the characteristics of the "classic" style of Greek art. It now awaits to consider the two millennia of ancient Greek architecture, to observe the various aspects it has taken, and how they relate to the "classic" form.

2 THE FORMS OF NATURE:

Stone Age to Homer: 4000–700 B.C.

Sometime around 2000 B.C. there began to appear in the Greek peninsula elements of a branch of the Indo-European folk of the regions to the north and north-east. These people spoke a language that linguistically is a phase in the direct development of the Greek of classical and modern times; their religion and basic institutions were in their essential character those of classical Greece. The classical Greeks and their culture were the result of a long development, with many infusions of other cultures and blood, that began as the invading Indo-Europeans encountered the previous inhabitants of the Aegean world.

The latter were already complex. Long before 3000 B.C. various peoples in a neolithic state of civilization had settled throughout the region from Thrace to Crete. It is impossible to speak with certainty about the distinctions among them; their architecture in particular is known only sporadically and presents, like their pottery, a variety of types, though less amenable to confident classification. For our purposes it is enough to observe that all the buildings known were probably houses, built of mud, mud-brick, small stones set in mud, reeds or brush with or without mud daubing and plastering. Circular, oval, apsidal, and rectangular buildings are known. Of the latter, some were essentially square (Plate 11), some oblong with the entrance at a short end, perhaps with a porch between projections of the side walls; such buildings occasionally had a similar "back porch" without an entrance. Normally these neolithic houses had only a single room, but sometimes there were more—rarely, however, more than two.

The date and slightness of the neolithic buildings make their connection with Greek architecture as such remote and difficult to assess. From the neolithic population in Crete, however, there developed during approximately the next thousand years a culture of much greater significance. Inhabiting a large and fertile island, well able to support a sizable population in comfort, isolated from the rest of the world and accessible only by the sea which they could easily control, the Minoan people developed a brilliant and sophisticated culture uniquely their own.

Minoan architecture was almost exclusively residential—there were no temples or public buildings properly speaking, and only a few monumental tombs. There are many private houses known from neolithic times up until Late Minoan III (around the thirteenth century), but the most conspicuous, and characteristic structures were the palaces of Middle Minoan III–Late Minoan II (1860–1400 B.C.), chiefly at Hagia Triada, Phaistos, Mallia, and, above all, Knossos (Plates 6-8, 10). The private houses were, typically, composed of a considerable number of rooms and were often more than one story high (Plate 9). To most of the rooms specific functions cannot be assigned, but it is of great significance that there were few if any interior courts or peristyle rooms, whereas light-wells were normal, opening onto certain interior rooms across their full width through an open screen of one or two columns or posts. Stairways were prominent features. The palaces seem to differ from this account notably in the great central courts around which the various apartments were built, but it is significant that the oldest palace, Knossos, began its existence as a town, with buildings in blocks around a square; the town became a palace by a more or less gradual process of consolidating all the buildings under one roof, except for the court, and covering even the streets to make them corridors. Among the functional units in the palace may be recognized the various districts of the original town: the long narrow storage chambers on the west, the shrines and ceremonial rooms facing along the west side of the court; the more luxurious living quarters off the south end of the east side of the court; service rooms and even small industries in the quarter north of this. Of these, the residential rooms are especially interesting, composed in adjoining volumes separated by slight piers that could be closed with screens or curtains, or by colonnades.[3]

The structural forms apart from solid walls were columns or piers. The columns were almost always smooth, and frequently smaller at the bottom than at the top—inverted tree trunks in inception, perhaps—bearing a wide flat echinus and broad abacus. The base, if any, was slight. The "piers" were in reality more of the order of doorframes. They were relatively narrow, seen from in front, supporting sections of walling rather than an architrave. Free porticoes of columns or true square piers may have lined a side of a courtyard.

The material of construction was relatively slight. Mud, mudbrick, small stones were common; wood was used occasionally in half-timber skeletons, and usually in columns. Ashlar blocks were used for foundation supports, wall-ends, or balustrades, seldom for walling in general save toward the end. The stone used was usually soft; gypsum was common.

Aesthetically, one outstanding peculiarity of the Minoan style was its preference for linear form—form in one dimension, so to speak. This is most obvious in the maze of narrow corridors which run all through the building, notably conspicuous, perhaps, to our eyes, in the major entrances at the southwest and northwest. It would have been conspicuous, too, in the long, low, and irregular profile of the building seen from the outside. Faience plaques depicting house fronts exist, suggesting that a three- or four-story façade was treated on the exterior in rectangular patterns developed from a wooden beam skeleton; but there is no indication of organization in three dimensions, and the major impression would have been created by the irregular skyline and groundline, and the swarm of lines produced by the variety of units in the façade and the various kinds of ornamentation. Even in large rooms lines of columns or piers or both, the openness of one or more walls, the several eccentric, conflicting lines of movement, would have diverted attention from the shape of the volume as such.

16

Closely related to linear form in the buildings was the volatile dynamic, the free movement. This resulted in part from the effect of the linear form itself and in turn helped to create linear form. Mobility was created also by the eccentricity of the arrangement —the lack of balance and concentrated dominance. Entrances were normally off-center; lines of movement through a volume were seldom on axis and usually involved a change in direction; frequently two or more such lines of movement intersected. The L-shape form characteristic of the colonnaded corridor at the end of the residential apartment was a frequent motif. If the Piano Nobile has been correctly restored, the "central Tri-Columnar Hall" (Plate 7) was a notable example of a restless complex of movements of lines of passage, lines of supports, opposition of different kinds of support, geometrical axes. Common was the arrangement of a column or pier on the axis of some opening—dividing, diverting movement to one side or another. The axial symmetry balance of the South Propylaea and Stair Hall was one of several exceptions, and, like most of them, late. The inverted tree-trunk column, stumpy as it sometimes was, nevertheless was less stable than one thickest at the base—its form is expansive rather than solid.

The mobility was supported by the general lack of regularity in the composition, and indeed by the kind of cohesion developed. Although at first glance it appears to be simply chaotic or accidental, the composition was in fact the natural result of the organic development of a town in its functional character. The unity was largely in the profusion, and in the simple, matter-of-fact accumulation of one thing with another as need arose. There was no superimposed formal organization, no structural logic, but there was the logic of use and direct response to the developing needs of living. In this sense the unity is "organic," "natural," and expresses the remarkable character of Minoan culture in its extraordinarily intimate relation to nature.

17

Meanwhile, on the mainland of Greece, an invading people had overrun a good part of the peninsula around 3000 B.C., overpowering and perhaps disrupting the neolithic civilization they encountered. The identity of these folk is not clear, and their culture is recognized by the arbitrary designation "Early Helladic." Their architecture is represented chiefly by relatively small houses constructed in the familiar mud and mud-brick, small stones, perhaps also reeds or brush—in form sometimes circular, sometimes rectangular. Two really substantial buildings are known: a rectangular structure at Lerna below Argos (Plate 12), and a circular building at nearby Tiryns (Plate 13). The building at Tiryns was about ninety-one feet in diameter: its foundations consist of a series of concentric circular rings with a row of tongue-like piers around the outside, but what form its super-structure took has never been reasonably conjectured. The plan of the building at Lerna[4] was, externally, a simple rectangle; within were two large rooms—that toward the front about twenty-two by twenty-seven feet—and several long narrow rooms or corridors. These buildings provide too little evidence for any elaborate account of the aesthetic character of the archi-tectural style of the period, but they possess a great deal of interest for certain technical details. Burnt brick was employed in some manner in the building at Tiryns; the interior surfaces of the walls of the building at Lerna were adorned with mud-plaster luxuriously textured with a comblike instrument, and it had a roof, probably with at least a slight pitch, of flat tiles, some of which were slate.

When the Hellenic peoples began to move into the Greek peninsula, then, they encountered and overpowered the Early Helladic folk on the mainland. During the Middle Helladic period, from about 2000 to about 1500, they appear to have remained fairly close to home. About 1600 their cultural devel-opment was dramatically accelerated, possibly because of in-creased contact—perhaps piratical—with Crete, or the shock of another wave of Hellenic invaders, or both. This development is signalized by the wealth of the Shaft Graves discovered by Heinrich Schliemann at Mycenae in 1876, and the related grave circle discovered there recently. The Late Helladic period, divided into several subdivisions on archaeological grounds, probably witnessed the arrival of still other contingents of Hellenes, the expansion of the consolidating Hellenic folk beyond the seas into Crete and even Cyprus, and the develop-ment of an increasingly rich and sophisticated civilization cen-tering in palaces at many of the great mythological sites of Greece, culminating most brilliantly at Mycenae around the thirteenth century.

The architecture of this people presents significant peculiari-ties. The functional forms include chiefly dwellings, but also tombs; again, almost nothing that could be called a temple, or a

18

"public building," has been identified with certainty. The dwellings ranged from private houses to the great palaces of the late days (Plates 21, 14, 17), but essential and characteristic was the megaron—a rectangular structure with the entrance at the middle of a short end, and a porch between the projecting side walls, facing on a court. These features were essential; in larger buildings there may have been a vestibule between the porch and the main room, and columns between the antae of the porch and supporting the roof of the hall. The megarons of Middle Helladic levels often had apsidal ends (Plate 21), and perhaps a room behind the hall, within the apse. In the palaces, the court may have had colonnades along one side or more, and a gate composed as an H-shaped structure with the door in the center of the crossbar and perhaps columns between the open ends. In the palaces especially, and even in smaller houses in the later phases, other rooms were accumulated around the megaron and its court.[5] The palaces in particular, taken as a whole, began to exhibit the general appearance of a Cretan palace, with long winding corridors and confused swarms of small rooms, but the courtyard always remained the particular appurtenance of the megaron, never the general focus of various apartments. In the later days, too, the palaces were fortified. Fortifications, to be sure, had been used for towns in Neolithic and Early Helladic times, but although the Mycenaean palaces often became so expansive as to resemble a town superficially, and even to include a protected retreat for elderly and ailing persons, the fortification remained part of a building—not of a community.

Hellenic burial places in the Middle Helladic period were simple graves sometimes of considerable size but having no visible form. But toward the end of the period, at least, they were arranged in plots marked above ground by circles of stones.[6] That this form ever achieved any formal monumentality may be doubted, but meanwhile other types of burial places were being developed: chamber tombs, rectangular in shape, cut out of the side of a hill and approached by a dromos—a narrow sloping trench; and tholos tombs—chambers circular in plan, domed in corbel vaulting like a "beehive" or egg, and also approached by a dromos. Although ultimately these tombs were splendidly built of fine masonry, with monumental door façades (Plate 16), it is fairly certain that they were never entered except for a funeral, and the dromos, perhaps even of the most monumental, was ordinarily filled up between funerals.

The materials employed for the smaller buildings and even extensively in the palaces were the familiar mud and stone and wood of the surrounding cultures, but especially in later days there developed a taste for dry-stone masonry on a large scale. Sometimes the blocks were but slightly dressed, sometimes they were well-squared ashlar.

In terms of aesthetics these Hellenic buildings had definite characteristics so far not observed in the Aegean world, unless in certain neolithic buildings. The rigorous axial symmetry of the megaron and propylon, with the related balanced dynamic, was important and in vivid contrast to the stubbornly eccentric focus and mobile dynamic of Minoan design. The Minoan influence, no doubt, may be seen in the subsidiary rooms of the palace, and in particular forms such as columns, and in the occasional arrangement of a column on axis as at Pylos (Plate 17) instead of two columns flanking the axis as in the normal megaron.[7] A certain idealism, in our technical sense, is evidenced by the great consistency in the form of the megaron wherever it appears, contrasting with the greater freedom in adapting shapes perceived elsewhere in the Aegean. One may sense also a tendency toward the aesthetic value of mass in the growing interest in heavy masonry (Plates 14, 15), and even in the compact shapes of the volumes of the megaron and other rooms. The composition of a palace as a whole is hardly conspicuous for regularity, nor is that of the megaron-courtyard-propylon complex; but the megaron and propylon themselves were composed in evenly distributed units. There was a preference for the principle of concentration in the dominance of the megaron over the other buildings around the court, in the minor accent of the propylon opposite, and in the formal development of entrances, as for example in the Lion Gate at Mycenae (Plate 15). A degree of architectonic cohesion in the disposition of units articulating movement from the entrance to the interior of the megaron at Tiryns may too be observed: a gate, a court, a gate, a court, the porch of the megaron, the vestibule, the hall—the whole more clearly constructed than anything at Knossos.

In short it seems abundantly clear that in the architecture of the Middle and Late Helladic period we find from the beginning some of the characteristics of classical design—simple at first, to be sure, but developing toward the later formulation, with non-Greek cultures offering and even pressing quite different principles upon it. Even from this relatively limited evidence, and certainly in the light of more abundant material found among ceramics, metalwork, frescoes, and the like (Plates 18, 19), one can form a general impression of more vigor and forthright directness among the Helladic than among the classic Hellenes; and one also sees a source of the warmer, more mobile vitality that in part distinguishes classic from Helladic.

The Aegean civilizations came to almost utter extinction around the eleventh century, following little-understood events reflected in the legends of the Trojan War and the Return of the Herakleidai—the "Coming of the Dorians." The succeeding centuries, until the eighth, are obscure to history; they saw, apparently, a shifting of the developing Hellenic peoples throughout the Aegean—into the eastern coast of Asia Minor—even to southern Italy and Sicily. Politically and economically the times were depressed, and life was surely agricultural, or pastoral, and not urban. Little is left in tradition or archaeology to clarify the picture. Pottery in some quantity reveals a continuity and slow development from Mycenaean to "Geometric" style (Plate 20) and to the age of Homer, but there are few architectural remains and these are too slight to be very illuminating.

One development is of real significance: buildings that may be regarded as temples made their appearance. Indeed, save for these there remains almost nothing else—even of private houses. These temples were simple structures of mud-brick or small stones and mud; both the rectangular and apsidal forms are known. Those on the mainland seem normally to have had the entrance on a short end; those in Crete, on a side. Some mainland buildings, to judge from terra-cotta models from Perachora and the Argive Heraeum (Plate 22), had porches with prostyle columns, but otherwise were open; these models also show a fashion for high peak roofs, perhaps normally of thatch. Rarely indeed was there more than one room in these structures.

Among these buildings are two of special importance. "Megaron B" at Thermon (Plate 21), dating from the ninth or eighth century, with a slightly curved rear wall and a slighter (unintentional?) curve on the side, had a small rear room or adyton, and, between the continuing side walls, a large front hall or porch open across the front. The first Heraeum at Samos, dating from about 775 (Plate 23), was also open across the front end; it had a single row of columns or posts down the middle, and three across the front between the antae. These buildings are

21

important for their hitherto unknown monumentality, for their extraordinarily long, narrow proportion, and for the fact that in each case, at a period after their original construction, they were provided with surrounding colonnades. At Thermon posts were erected in a continuous hairpin plan along the sides and around the back of the building, while a straight row of posts stretched across the front. This suggests that in its original conception the "peripteron" was not integrally part of the temple, but an addition—an attachment for the protection of an area in some sense separate from the essential building.

As a naos—a living space—would not be provided for a "god" until such a being, integrated, localized, self-embodied, rather than a pervasive numinous power, was conceived by men, we would infer that the first appearance of the simple naos as a "temple" was the direct response to a new conception of deity beginning to take form after the collapse of Mycenaean culture. The addition of a protected volume external to the naos of the god would then in its turn derive from needs external to the god —those of the people attending on his worship.[8] Thus, the evidence, slight though it is, is important to show the continuity through the period, and the first simple responses, in "natural" ways, to the stirring of new needs.

3   THE FORM OF SUBSTANCE:

Homer to Plato: 700–400 B.C.

By the end of the eighth century powerful economic, social, and intellectual forces had begun to engender far-reaching results in molding the character of Greek culture. Among the most significant are the burst of trade throughout the Mediterranean, especially with Egypt and Asia; the growth of the characteristic Greek political institution, the city-state; and a social revolution from landed aristocracy through commercial and proletarian oligarchy and tyranny to the more refined forms of Athenian democracy. In another area we see the development of literary style from the powerful surging flow of Homeric epic, through the briefer pieces of Hesiod and the lyric poets treating expansively and more personally some aspect of life, to the studies of human experience in depth in the complex, compact drama and history of Sophocles and Thucydides in the fifth century. In still another, we see intellectual interest ranging from the descriptive summarizing catalogues of data in Hesiod, through the study of the very nature of being and physical substance among the pre-Socratic philosophers, to the rigorous effort of Plato to comprehend form itself as ultimate reality. These centuries were animated with confidence–with the conviction that man could comprehend and achieve his proper ends, and need fear only stepping beyond his proper sphere. For this effort there was energy and resource abundantly available, and it was fully employed.

The climax came in the mainland of Greece in the fifth century for particular reasons. The Persian wars, which involved Asia Minor and Greece itself through the first quarter of the century, left the states of Asia Minor in a condition of uncertainty, as the Persian Empire still lay at the frontier and its presence was constantly felt. In Greece, on the other hand, there had been decisive victory, resulting in the disappearance of actual danger together with the surge of an exultant sense of irrepressible power in having thrown back a superior foe. The sudden self-confidence led the Athenians to embark on a tremendous war with their rivals, the Spartans, and maintain the effort in spite of heavy loss. The stimulus of these circumstances came at a moment of maximum resources and when the goals of the interest of previous generations were in sight. It was a natural culmination.

In architecture many types of buildings fulfilling the new requirements appeared through these three centuries, beginning with the seventh–sporadically, initially, but in increasing numbers later on. Temples were abundant from the seventh century, at first largely in the form of the simple cella, soon predominantly in the peripteral form of the Hephaisteion. The simpler forms continued also as dedications and "treasuries"–storehouses for dedications at large sanctuaries. Stoas may have been more abundant than remains suggest, never losing their essential form of a colonnade in front of a wall, with the intervening volume covered. There were some assembly halls for religious or political needs. Sanctuaries were elaborated with such buildings, though the bare essential was simply an altar–and a processional way. A few houses are known.

Materials for temples in the seventh century, for other buildings through the sixth, and for houses through the fifth, were the familiar mud-brick, mud and stone, and wood, but for temples from the end of the seventh century and for other buildings increasingly limestone or marble in ashlar masonry appeared and became standard. A notable new material was terra cotta, baked tile, for roofing and the ornamental antefixes and the like (Plates 33a, b). It was also often used for elaborate akroteria for the corners and peaks of gables. In the earliest phases it was occasionally used even for metopes or triglyphs.

The functional forms of structure included not only the Doric order, described typically in the Hephaisteion, but the Ionic, which was developed early in Asia Minor (Plates 45, 46). The Ionic column usually had a base, deeper and more boldly separated flutes, a characteristic capital consisting of a scroll-like element lying across an ornamented echinus on top of the shaft, an architrave with three fasciae, and either a frieze or a row of square blocks called dentils below the cornice. During the seventh century another type of column was known whose capital, the "Aeolic," was conceived rather as a flowering or branching of the stem of the shaft, with leaves rolling out from around the top; and still another capital of volute-like forms developed from a bifurcation of the top of the shaft, spreading and coiling under the architrave (Plate 28).

By the seventh century there were at least a few buildings which reflected the surge of a new and imaginative style. The Temple of Apollo at Thermon (Plate 21) had a peripteron of wooden columns or posts—five on the front and fifteen on the side. This is in a notably long, narrow proportion, and the single row of columns down the middle of the naos further accentuates the linear concept. The Heraeum at Olympia (Plate 35), also had wooden columns on the exterior, six on the front, sixteen on the side; inside there were projecting buttresses or attached columns along each wall. Nothing can be known about these columns and hence about the vertical proportions in the building, but some stone columns from the late seventh century in the Marmaria at Delphi were unusually long and thin, with thin, wide-spreading echini (Plate 29). Earlier than any of these the second Heraeum at Samos (Plate 24) was also long—6 × 18—with attached columns on the wall inside the naos, but the second row of columns or posts across the front created a volume transverse to the main axis, as well as a second façade in the progression toward the interior, restraining momentarily the flow of volume longitudinally and emphasizing the lateral dimension. The Temple of Artemis at Garitsa in Corfu (Kerkyra, Corcyra) (Plate 30) was perhaps the oldest known temple completely of stone. It was remarkable in being octastyle—eight columns on the front—and pseudodipteral (there being space equivalent to that needed for a row of columns between the outer colonnade and the naos). Moreover its pediment was adorned with sculptures whose exuberance, expressed in richly textured and patterned surfaces, gives some ground for a sense of the aesthetic qualities that were probably desired in the building as a whole (Plate 31, and compare 32).

In the Aegean islands and Asia Minor a number of important buildings from the seventh century were not peripteral. At Naeandria (Plate 25) a broadly proportioned structure on an even broader platform retained the longitudinal emphasis of a central row of columns in the interior in spite of its entrance at the middle of an end. At Prinias in Crete a similarly broadly proportioned building even had a support on axis between the antae of the porch (Plates 26, 27). The flat forms of the "Aeolic" capitals from Naeandria and related buildings, like Larisa and Kolumdado (Plate 28), and of the sculptured lintel and square supporting members at Prinias, again reveal the affection for luxurious surface with evident lingering of the taste for free linear movement itself.

In the sixth century stone temples appear in great abundance throughout the Greek world. It was an age of experiment in all aspects of design, and there is great variety from time to time and place to place—as well as within particular localities.

The variety of adjustments and proportions in the arrangement of volumes becomes apparent from a comparison of the plans of buildings of the period throughout the Greek world (Plates 34, 35, 36, and note 9), although imperfect information about vertical dimensions leaves our conception incomplete. In some, the naos and its proper subsidiary volumes remained distinct from the enclosing volume of the peripteron: the effect, however, was the reverse of the primitive one assumed for the peripteron *added around* the naos of Megaron B at Thermon (Plate 21)—rather it was the effect of a building *within* the enclosure of outer columns and roof. In others, the columns of the pronaos were contrived to integrate the interior forms with the outer, by interlocking and mutually related forms and structures. In all of these the integrity of each volume in itself, as one in a chain or progression of several, or as a channel of movement in itself, would be maintained. But in the designs of the great dipteral buildings of Asia Minor (cf. Plate 36 and note 9), the ranks and files of columns, receding in every direction, would have created a generalized expanse in which the solids and volumes of the naos were homogeneous elements in the continuum; and even the long narrow volume between each pair of rows of columns, blending with its neighbors in the rippled texture of the total volume, would have lost some of its longitudinal force.[9]

The major longitudinal movement of volumes was emphasized in western buildings by an extra room in the rear, usually called an adyton, and in some buildings was further elaborated by elevating one or more of the successive stages above the one in front, so that the worshiper ascended, as he approached the image, from volume to volume. The distinction in level was seldom great, of course, but when at all present would have constituted a real factor. The low—two-step—platform of the third Heraeum at Samos, with the colonnade drawn back some ten feet from the edge, and the high platform of the fourth Heraeum, would have created special effects of this sort.

The solid elements of the buildings of the sixth century, too, had considerable variety. The columns (Plates 30, 37-39, 42), in general, from the beginning of the century were notably short in proportion to their thickness, and in the Doric order, at least, had a pronounced diminution; many of them had pronounced entasis—curvature of the vertical profile—also, but lacked the more subtle refinements. The bases of the Ionic order were large with sweeping profiles, and elaborately textured with grooving or other ornament (Plate 45). Doric capitals showed a general chronological progression from broadly flaring, sweeping curves to a more compact conical form (Plates 29, 30, 37–39, 41, 42). Ionic capitals also spread broadly (Plate 46), with bold shallow bulging forms rather than the crisp concave hollows of the later classical manner. Especially in Magna Graecia moldings of Ionic character were applied to the Doric column and anta capitals—for example, leaf-moldings under the capital, subduing the transition from shaft to echinus (though not obscuring it) and contributing another texture to the design (Plate 41).

The columns, usually low and close-set by classical standards, developed a strong horizontal movement in the facade and especially on the flanks. This motion was smooth and flowing, but there was variety in the spacing of the columns in Doric buildings, particularly in response to a problem created by the relation of the column to the triglyphs in the frieze.

The triglyph at a corner, being narrower than the thickness of a column, would lie some distance within the corner of the

27

frieze, if its center fell on the axis of the column. Thus the absolute regularity of spacing of columns and of triglyphs could not be maintained simultaneously, if it were desired to have the triglyph full on the corner. It is possible, of course, to harmonize the discrepancy by compromising a little on the absolute regularity of all components throughout their entire expanse, without apparent violence to any, but the solutions of the sixth century did work perceptible violence on one or another of the components, thus introducing a note of irregularity or strain in one or another of the rhythms.

But the most conspicuous peculiarity of temple design in the sixth century was in the entablature, in the broadest sense—the parts above the columns (Plates 30, 39, 40, 43). In this period this part of the façade occupied generally a much larger proportion of the composition than in later periods, with the result that the colonnade was less open, while the flat expanse of masonry above was prominent as enclosing wall and far less distinct as an aspect of the ceiling and roofing elements. Thus the façade became a continuous plane, variously textured but essentially one unit; while the existence of the over-all three-dimensional form of the building, that would be emphasized by the sharp distinction of a capping element, was minimized. This effect was at its maximum in a few buildings such as the temple of Athena (Ceres) at Paestum (Plate 39), which had no horizontal cornice in front, so that the triangle of the pediment merged almost unimpeded with frieze and architrave and the sweep of columns below.

This great expanse of solid masonry above the columns was treated with considerable variety. In most Doric temples the basic pattern of architrave and frieze was employed, but with much variety in the minor details. The number of guttae on regulae and mutules was sometimes less than six; the mutules between the triglyphs were sometimes narrower than those over the triglyphs (Plates 30, 40); sometimes, as in the Temple of Athena (Ceres) at Paestum (Plate 39), other kinds of moldings than the normal Doric appeared above architrave and frieze. The variations were among buildings, of course, and the system was consistent in any one building, but the significance is, first, that in this as in other points of design there was a moderate degree of particularism; and even more, in any one building employing a variation on the ideal, the rhythms and patterns would be variegated and intricate as the meters of contemporary lyric poetry were.

The colors of the elements of the entablature (Plate 40), moreover, bolder than later, accentuated the beats of the rhythms and the range of texture. The sculpture, too, in pediments and metopes was brilliantly painted according to its own canons; the lights and shadows among the figures, the increasingly intricate patterns of movement in the sculptured figures added greatly to the richness of the surface of the façade. Finally the great terra-cotta acroteria and other ornamental tiles brought along the top of the building bold surfaces with lavish, almost extravagant colors and textures (Plates 33a, b).

In all this it may appear that the originality and curiosity of the sixth century was mostly in Asia Minor and even more in Magna Graecia, for the buildings of mainland Greece—the Temple of "Apollo" at Corinth (Plates 35, 38), the Old Athena Temple at Athens, the Doric and Ionic treasuries at Delphi (Plates 43, 44)—are all, within a moderate range of variation, closer to the "conservative" main stream of design and proportions, as we are likely to think of it, which runs through the fifth century. Actually, the individuality of the mainland style within the sixth century is nonetheless real for the fact that it was followed into the fifth. The "mutation" of the sixth century that was "successful," so to speak, was that of the mainland. Its success was due in part to the fact that in it the formulation of volumes and solids was best adapted to three-dimensional form —that is, to the form in which geometrical mass is most clearly perceptible—and in it could be developed the clearest architectonic organization permeated with the most effective currents of regular rhythmic movement. In part its success was also due to the stimulus of the destruction of the Persian Wars, dramatically commemorated by the arrangement, in the new fortifications of the Acropolis in Athens, of the column drums and other members of archaic buildings on the Acropolis destroyed by the Persians.

In this tradition the Hephaisteion, which we have already described at some length, was typical (Plates 2-5). Essentially similar, with differences important only in a detailed analysis of Greek architecture, would be the Temples of Aphaia at Aegina (Plate 51), Zeus at Olympia, Poseidon at Sunion, Nemesis at Rhamnous (these last two were erected by the same architect as the Hephaisteion's and differed only in the most subtle ways) —even temples in Magna Graecia such as those of Poseidon at Paestum (Plate 52), Concord at Akragas, "A" at Selinus.

More revealing than the differences among such temples are those between the Hephaisteion and the buildings on the Athenian Acropolis. The Parthenon (Plates 53-56, 64) shows the limit and nature of possible modification of the ideal type if all external controls were removed: it was conceived as the supreme architectural adornment of a city that at the time was supreme in the Greek world, at the height of all its resources.[10] Whatever the architect—and the people—might have desired in a building might have been provided, or at least attempted. In fact, nothing more than a moderately and subtly enriched version of the type represented by the Hephaisteion was considered—though completely and perfectly realized. The over-all proportions are essentially the same so that, although the Parthenon is more than twice as large, it is no more dominating, and the difference in size is most effectively revealed in the 8 × 17 colonnade of the Parthenon compared with the 6 × 13 of the Hephaisteion. In the Parthenon the columns are a little more compact, the entablature a little heavier. The building is richer in having all metopes sculptured rather than only those on the front and at the ends of the sides, with a frieze running all around the top of the cella wall inside rather than merely across the pronaos; and, of course, it is infinitely richer through the effect of light and shadow, movement and texture of the sculptures themselves. But all this, in a sense, is simply a function of the greater scale and is no more obtrusive in proportion. There are, however, important differences in the adaptation of naos to peripteron: the prostyle façade of six columns across the very shallow pronaos creates a recession of shallow volumes in the organization of movement from the exterior to the interior, instead of offering the more spacious volumes with greater penetration encountered in entering the Hephaisteion. But the most significant differences are scarcely perceptible: the curvatures of steps and stylobate, architrave and frieze; the intricate system of inclinations of the columns on front, sides and corners, in addition to the finer quality of the more common refinements of entasis and the extraordinary precision of carving, even in such minute details as the scarcely noticeable arrises between the flutes. The great superiority of the Parthenon, then, lies in the sheer quality and sensitivity in the multitude of details, any of which belong in any building, but all of which are embodied in this building, to animate it within its logically structured regularity more pervasively and more completely than any other building. The result stimulates most fully and exactly the sensory realization of the Hellenic concept of the good.

Revealing in another way is the Erechtheum (Plates 53, 57-59, 64), which shows the extent to which the ideal forms could yield to drastic external controls—not economic, to be sure, but topographical and cultic.

Several cults were accommodated in the building: in the eastern part was the most holy shrine of Athena Polias; in the western part were shrines of vague figures from early mythic tradition—Erechtheus and Butes, and the obscurely related Poseidon and Hephaistos. Within the western part was the "sea" of Poseidon; just outside, but within the north porch, were marks of Poseidon's trident on the rock; outside to the west were the sanctuary of Pandrosos and the numinous olive tree of Athena; under the southwest corner was the tomb of Cecrops. The building, accommodated to these *sacra* and distributed over an irregular terrain, had to have an east entrance at one level, a secondary entrance at the west end of the south side at the same level, a major entrance at the west end of the north side at a distinctly lower level, a secondary entrance on the west at the same low level. For the two major entrances—on east and north —normal Ionic façades were designed. That for the east was of the usual shallow prostyle kind; that on the north was a semi-independent open porch on a scale consonant with the double height of the building as erected from the lower level. The entrance from the west was a simple, almost unadorned door conceived as leading to a basement, with the main floor level above designated by a colonnade resting on the basement wall. The entrance from the south was built with a small porch enclosed by a balustrade supporting caryatids carrying the roof—a more original design than any of the other porches, but with precedents—so far as the caryatids are concerned, at least—in the richer small buildings of the archaic period. In short, the solution to the problem was not so much to force all the particulars into one scheme, nor yet to yield to each in its eccentricities, but to admit the particular freely in its natural place, recognizing it in its ideal form.

Finally the Propylaea[11] (Plates 53, 60-64), too, shows the adaptation of an ideal form—in this case the form of a gate—to a particular situation, in two ways. First, in the original design the essential form of the gate was preserved, richer, again, in its complication of volumes and its quality of workmanship than

31

most gates, but still remaining typical. Second, even in its existing, curtailed, and unfinished state, the parts actually executed constitute completed forms, fulfilled in themselves according to the ideal types.

Thus in the temples of the seventh through the fifth centuries the gradual achievement of an agreement, after exploration of various values, on the kind of form most fully illustrated today in the Hephaisteion seems to be seen. It is not necessary to repeat the introductory analysis of that building at this point, but it may be valuable to look briefly at the elements of the Ionic order, not exemplified in the Hephaisteion: the bases, shafts, capitals, and moldings of the Erechtheum, (Plate 59), the Propylaea (Plate 62, 63), the temple of Athena Nike (Plate 63). These, too, in comparison with their counterparts of the archaic period (Plates 44-46), show the same ideal, objective, and literal conception of a reality that is not only clear, substantial, alive, but also evenly and logically structured (compare Plate 50).

Buildings other than temples may have existed through these centuries in greater numbers than are now known, lost because they were constructed of slighter materials. Certainly in the Heraeum at Samos a large stoa was built in the seventh century (Plate 24), elaborated to the extent of having a double row of columns (really posts), and being divided into three sections or "rooms."[12] In this the essential functional and aesthetic purposes of the stoa are already fully achieved: to create an interior volume freely related to an exterior volume which is to a degree created, in two dimensions, by the breadth of the stoa itself and, subjectively, in the third, by the implications of movement toward and away from the façade and the interior of the building. More famous is the smaller, simpler marble Ionic stoa of the Athenians at Delphi of the early fifth century. By the end of the fifth century monumental stoas in stone devoted to purposes reflecting the full range of potential function existed. On the Acropolis the architecture of the Sanctuary of Artemis of Brauron (Plates 53, 64) consisted exclusively of a simple stoa with long narrow wings projecting from each end to enclose the space on three sides: the walls of these wings were treated with half-columns.[13] In the agora (Plates 65, 66), the Stoa of Zeus was much finer in conception and execution, with a double colonnade and temple-like façades projecting from each end—providing the building itself with significant dominants in its own dynamic balance. On the south side of the agora was a stoa less rich in material and refined in execution, having not only a double colonnade but a series of rooms behind—these devoted, remarkably enough, to dining rooms, presumably for civic officials and guests of the city.[14]

Stoas were used even for gatherings of considerable groups of people—the Stoa of Zeus at Athens may have served as the courtroom for King Archon—but other types of buildings were required for larger groups and other specific purposes. It is characteristic that many of these were unroofed, open-air enclosures. The conspicuous example of this is the theater which, however, did not begin to have formal shape until the end of the fifth century. The earliest arrangements for dramatic or quasi-dramatic purposes required simply a slope of ground—if that—facing on the place of the performance. This was, originally, before the development of drama as an independent art, some religious rite, and the "theatron"—seeing place—might be simply the slope of the hill beside a temple. Even after the drama began to develop independently in the cult of Dionysos, around the end of the sixth century, the same accommodation sufficed; any construction was limited to temporary affairs of light materials for the housing of costumes and properties; before this lay the orchestra—the "dancing place"—and beyond was the hillside with seating accommodation, whether natural or contrived. Not until around the middle of the century was the scene building constructed of even semi-permanent material, though its function remained the same—storage, and a façade before which the action in the orchestra or on a low stage between could take place. Aesthetically these buildings depended more on the natural setting and the dramatic production than on architectura design.

For smaller groups, or those requiring seclusion, an assembly hall was occasionally provided. Thus a simple apsidal structure housed the council at Olympia in the early sixth century; shortly before the middle of the century the council at Athens was provided with a crude rectangular room facing on a large open enclosure, at the other end of which was a building consisting of a number of rooms facing on a court, lined on two sides with wooden posts, stoa-fashion; this latter building served to house the prytany—the "executive committee" of the council during its continuous service of a month (Plate 48).

What came to be the typical form of assembly hall was developed early at Eleusis for the secret rites of Demeter (Plate 47). Originally the rites were performed in the open air around the shrine; ultimately a building was erected to include the shrine

33

and seclude the participants. It was rectangular—longer than wide, with a porch across one end, but in the fifth century the first of a series of much larger square buildings was projected and ultimately built. There were seats running along the walls, and the roof was supported on parallel rows of columns, creating a hypostyle hall. In this the interior volume was essentially cubical, organized only in the rhythm of ranks and file of columns. In Athens the Council House of the late sixth century was of this type, and so, too, its later fifth-century replacement (Plate 65), though this was modified by the semicircular arrangement of seats within, achieving for the first time an architectural design comprising the fusion of square and circle in one form. The Odeion of Pericles, south of the Acropolis, was square—the arrangement of seats and columns probably rectangular—and was famous in antiquity for its roof, which may have been pyramidal. A peculiar form of assembly hall is the fifth-century Tholos at Athens (Plate 65), a cylindrical structure with solid walls and six columns within, arranged not in a ring concentric with the walls but in two facing arcs creating a sort of aisle along the diameter. Parallels for this may well have existed but are not known for the "tholoi" of the archaic period at Delphi were not assembly halls and were designed with peripteral colonnades.

It is, then, noteworthy that there were so few enclosed buildings, although this may have social and functional explanations. As to those that existed, it is significant that they were restricted to the most simple geometric forms, and indicate no effort to elaborate the form. The bare essential form for the purpose at hand was created, in and of itself.

Finally domestic architecture should be noted. From Larisa in Asia Minor (Plate 49) sixth-century houses are known which follow the forms of the Mycenaean megaron. A "megaron" type almost surely existed in Greece itself during the eighth century, since this scheme was followed in the naos of the temple, and the terra-cotta models from Perachora and the Argive Heraeum may as well be houses as temples. In these the aesthetic principles were essentially the same as in the Mycenaean megaron. But on the mainland an entirely different type seems to have been favored in the fifth century, characterized by an irregular agglomeration of quadrangular rooms around an open courtyard (Plate 67). Aesthetically it is marked by the irregularity, and the fact that the rooms have no relation to each other—all are entered from the courtyard, each exists as a unit of its own.

Moreover, the rooms, and the courtyard too, were relatively small and compact.

Concluding this view of the classical phase of Greek architecture with a reference to the manner of planning groups of buildings, one is immediately struck by a lack of logical order in the arrangement of sanctuary or public market (Plates 53, 64, 65, 106-108) that seems fundamentally incompatible with the thorough ordering and simple geometry of the buildings themselves. It is true that the so-called Hippodameian system of town planning, in rectangular blocks of streets, was being developed during the fifth century, and even in the archaic periods in the new foundations of colonies in the west, such as in Selinus, even temples were lined up in parallel rows. Still, the typical composition of groups through the fifth century with its lack of formal order does demand an accounting. In fact this irregularity accomplishes two results, whether from conscious intent or not. First, it makes each building an independent reality existing in its own right, and second, it relieves the careful definition in the buildings themselves. On the one hand the order in the building is the more evident by contrast; on the other, the casual movement of the exterior space, the variety of natural and monumental elements around, create a freedom and vividness of their own which strengthen the elements of vitality within the building. The totality, then, creates and embodies an awareness of objective reality, structurally ordered but alive; a part of the world, to be sure, but free and self-sufficient within it (compare Plate 50).

4   THE FORM OF KOSMOS:
Plato to Augustus: 400–31 B.C.

In the fifth century man's potentialities were defined by the tangible limits of the city-state; in the Hellenistic period, within the vastly expanded horizon of the world of affairs, the boundaries of his sphere lay far beyond his objective experience. In the fifth century philosophers were still concerned with essential substance; later, beginning with Plato and Aristotle, they struggled with problems of intangibles—metaphysical, ethical, and physical relationships. Before, religion was a meeting of man with god and divine law; after, it was increasingly a matter of making them one. In literature and art the perspective shifts from a concentration on man in his direct experience, to man in his experience of psychic and environmental forces. The external phenomena which accompany this change in ethos—whether as cause or effect—include the failures of the city-state during the Peloponnesian Wars and their aftermath, the conquest of the east by Alexander, and the subsequent establishment of the Hellenistic kingdoms. The shift began within the Hellenic world, but soon merged in a confluence of cultures throughout the eastern Mediterranean, and ultimately also with the Roman tradition, which spread finally to the limits of the Mediterranean world under Augustus Caesar.

In architecture, too, this period saw changes. To be sure there were no important new structural devices. Arches, known perhaps even earlier, and even vaulting were employed, but not to any extent or with any aesthetic importance. Nor were any essentially new functional forms developed, although forms known before but rarely or in incipient form become common and more varied. Particularly noteworthy is the gymnasium, and the smaller palaestra, essentially rectangular open areas for exercise enclosed by colonnades, behind which on some sides might be enclosed rooms including baths, dressing rooms, lecture halls. Increasingly important was a type of religious building, completely enclosed, designed for private worship by initiates in some "mystery" cult. Normally it would resemble a house, with a large colonnaded courtyard off which opened the cult chambers, including one or more rooms for the image of the god or gods, a banqueting hall, and special rooms for the particular rites of the cult. Such buildings existed in earlier periods, but the societies using them were relatively small and their establishments poor and vaguely defined, in contrast to the much greater prominence of this kind of cult in Hellenistic times.[15]

The number of large temples in the traditional forms dating from the fourth century are fewer in proportion to those of the fifth and sixth, and fewer still during the Hellenistic period. This is in some part due to the great number then surviving from earlier years and also to the spread of the new religions, but also may be due in some part at least to the limitation of the power of the traditional forms to embody the new values. There is, however, a shift in emphasis in the design of such temples as were erected, especially in those which were actually new designs and not simply reconstructions of older buildings.

For one thing, a greater emphasis was put on the vertical dimension. This was achieved in part by a fairly consistent shortening of the proportions of the ground plan (Plate 69). During the fifth century this would have been in a ratio with the length slightly more than twice the width; later the length would be slightly less than twice the width. Concurrently there was a tendency to make columns taller in proportion to their thickness than hitherto, emphasizing the vertical movement as well as adding actual height. Also, the proportion of entablature to the total expanse of the façade was reduced, lessening the force of the entablature in terminating the upward movement; the consequence of this in a Doric frieze extended to the introduction of an extra triglyph in each intercolumniation, complicating the rhythms and textures and lightening the weight of the entablature in general. The tendency, then, is to diminish the mass of the building (Plates 70-72).

The effect was felt too in the volumes. Even in regular peripteral temples the proportion of the thickness of the column to the intercolumniation was diminished, giving greater prominence to the empty space and the potential of movement through it. Moreover, many major buildings were built on the pseudo-peripteral scheme—that is, with the space between naos wall and outer colonnade double the normal width found in regular temples. This was the form of some archaic buildings, but in them the height was less, and the volume relatively low and flat in contrast to the greater height that was characteristic of the great temple at Sardis begun in the fourth century, the third-century temples at Messa and Sminthe, and the second-century Artemesium at Magnesia (Plates 68, 69, 71). The effect in these was to emphasize the seclusion of the naos within the open space enclosed by the peripteron, and to maximize the openness—the width and height, as well as length, of the colonnade corridors themselves. The peculiar compositions of interior volumes in the temples at Sardis, and Miletus, and the development of the naos and pronaos of the Artemesium at Magnesia, are further indication of a growing interest in problems of relationship of volumes.

Finally it is worth noting the number of temples on elevated platforms, approached by considerable numbers of steps. This too may well have been adapted from archaic buildings like the Fourth Heraeum at Samos, but in any case the temples at Sardis, Ephesus, Miletus, and Magnesia did stand high on all sides and, whether by accident or choice, some small temples like that of Hera Basileia at Pergamum also stood in elevated position approached only from the front. All this relates to a growing interest in intangibles, like volume, space-time relationships, and freer, fuller movement.

The new interest is evident, also, in the Corinthian capital, which appeared first in the latter part of the fifth century at

Bassae as a tightly compact form. In the Tholos in the Marmaria at Delphi around 400 B.C. (Plate 73) the volutes were independent reverse spirals applied to the bell supporting the abacus at the corners. At Tegea (Plate 74), the interior half columns about mid-century had low compact capitals but the leaves began to flare and the volutes to grow up from their midst. In the capitals of the Choregic Monument of Lysikrates a few years later (Plate 76) the leaves and especially volutes had an almost detached form, similar to applied metal work. In the Tholos at Epidaurus, the leaves were looser, the volutes more slender and volatile (Plate 75), and it was this form which prevailed; the developed form of the capitals of the Olympieion at Athens in the second century were conceived of leaves and volutes, each of diminished intrinsic importance, growing and spreading one from behind the other, and reaching into the space around in luxuriant profusion (Plate 77).

Ionic bases and capitals, too, and the traditional moldings of egg-and-dart, bead-and-reel, and various kinds of leaves—broad and flat in the sixth century, solid and compact in the fifth—were now set in ample space bringing light and shadow more fully into play and emphasizing the space itself as an element in the relationship (Bases: Plates 45, 63, 80; Capitals: Plates 46, 60, 81; Moldings: Plates 44, 59, 78-79).

But it is rather the stoas which represent the new age, both functionally and aesthetically. One of the finest was the South Stoa at Corinth,[16] from the latter part of the fourth century (Plates 82, 83). Though built of poros—a relatively soft limestone—the workmanship was in every way of the highest quality, and the exposed surfaces were covered, as poros buildings usually were, with a white, thin, hard, and smooth stucco or plaster which could take and hold the most refined detail. It was some one hundred sixty-five meters in length, stretching almost the entire length of the agora. Along the front ran a narrow terrace; then there was a façade of the Doric order, and a row of Ionic columns down the middle of the covered space behind; the rear half was devoted to a series of two-room shop spaces on the ground level and another above, presenting a two-story façade within the building facing on the open colonnade-space, about twelve meters wide. The open floor space, almost 40 feet wide —about 22,000 square feet—and some 23 feet high, was extremely spacious and allowed the free circulation of large numbers of people.

The variety of stoas in their adaptation to particular use—
without altering fundamentally the aesthetic form—was almost
infinite. Some were simple—a row of columns before a wall;
others consisted of a double row of columns before a wall; others
had single or double rows of rooms behind the colonnades.
Many were but a single story in height; some were more than
one, in various combinations. The Stoa of Attalos at Athens
(Plates 84-87), from the mid-second century, had the colonnade
as well as the shops in two stories.[17] At Assos (Plate 88) was a
four-story stoa—though its principle façade, on the Agora, was
only one story in height, the other three being below this and
facing (not with colonnades) on the hill slope below.

Other kinds of adaptation existed. The Middle Stoa along the
south side of the main area of the Agora in Athens (Plate 110),
from around the middle of the second century, had no walls at
all: there were columns on all four sides, and a row running down
the middle, between which screens could be arranged to develop
spatial arrangements suitable to changing needs. Southward
from the east end of this, enclosing the smaller "Commercial
Agora" on the east, was a short double-facing stoa fronting
both on the road to the east and on the Commercial Agora
behind: in the middle of its central wall was a more or less
monumental doorway, so that the whole building became a kind
of propylon or formal entrance. At the other extreme there were
stoas—if they may be so called—that were completely enclosed,
with no exterior columns.

These stoas were independent buildings, self-defined, one unit
with the terrace which normally lies in front of them. They were
related to the space in front as one integral thing to another;
though they helped to define that space, they were distinct from
it. A somewhat different relationship existed in the U-shaped
stoas of the cities of Asia Minor, for example Priene and Miletus
(Plates 89-91). Here the stoa, itself relatively simple, was drawn
along three sides of the open area so as to confine the area almost
entirely—not quite completely, for the fourth side was open to
the street and the more dominant stoa beyond. L-shaped stoas,
too, were known, with a still different relationship between
building and space, but with the U-shape stoa the semienclosed
space became a fixed and integral element in an architectural
unit.

Yet another scheme of relationships was created in a building
such as the Roman Market in Athens[18] (Plate 92) or the Stoa of

40

the Italians at Delos (Plate 93, upper left), where the colonnades ran around all four sides and the space was completely isolated. Such an enclosure was in effect a building in which the enclosed volume was a peristyle courtyard—a whole and separate unit among other units, whereas in the composition of a U-shaped stoa the space, though articulated with the building, retained contact with the space beyond, and remained part of it.

The stoa, then, became a device for creating an interior volume that was integrated in various degrees with an external volume—as the peripteral temple integrated a solid form to the world about it. The forms of volume predominated in the stoa, though they remained the simple rectangular prisms that characterized the earlier solids and volumes. The forms of solids themselves are little changed, save that they are lighter individually. In over-all composition, the chief difference from the earlier style is in the more even, general distribution, and the lack of boldly focused dominants.

The concept of creating an open volume as the essential part of a building, characteristic of the Roman Market in Athens, as distinct from out-of-door space drawn into an architectural composition, was characteristic also of the gymnasium and palaestra (Plate 94). The fully enclosed rooms were independent entities, connected only with the colonnaded corridor, and definitely subsidiary to the open area. The seclusion of the enclosed space, its self-containment, and yet its complete openness to the sky above, together with the simplicity of the expanse of the colonnades, the lightness of their structure and proportion constitute its peculiar aesthetic quality.

Completely enclosed halls appeared in greater numbers and variety and increased in sophistication. In the mid-fourth century was erected the Thersilion at Megalopolis, remarkable chiefly in that its colonnaded porch served as the scene, or perhaps rather proskenion, of the theater beyond, a rare example of the fusion of two distinct buildings into one aesthetic and functional composition. It was rectangular, a little wider than deep, and the internal supports were arranged in lines parallel to the back and side walls but so that they all fell on lines radiating from a point near the middle. There were, however, so many supports that it is likely that this system was not easily perceptible. A large enclosed building—sometimes called a "stoa" or a "basilica" or less controversially a "hypostyle hall"—is known from the harbor region in Delos from around 210 B.C. (Plate 93, lower left). The structure, a large rectangle with one long side open for most of its length through a colonnade, may in fact have been a warehouse or auction building, and in a sense had little architectural pretension, but it did have many peculiarities in details inside and outside. The roof was supported on columns, arranged so that there were four Ionic columns on axis (a space in the middle of the row, where a fifth might have stood, was vacant); around this was a rectangle of Ionic columns; around that a rectangle of Doric columns. Thus the volumes were concentric rectangular prisms. Much finer buildings from the point of view of material and workmanship were the Ekklesiasterion at Priene (Plates 95, 96) and the Bouleuterion at Miletus (Plate 91, center), representative of two developed types of a small assembly hall. The former had seats arranged parallel to three walls, the speakers' platform on the fourth; the latter had seats in concentric semicircles, as in a theater.

The design of theaters changed notably during this period. In the fourth century, the theater at Epidaurus (Plate 97) was developed from a fully circular orchestra; the seats rose in concentric semicircles from the orchestra and were divided by radiating narrow-stepped aisles of ascent and descent. The scene building was presumably a simply designed structure of rectangular forms, probably two stories in height with a one-story proskenion stretched across the front of it, and slightly projecting wings at each end. The roof of the proskenion could be reached by ramps from each side, or from within the scene building, but it was probably not used much for acting; the acting still normally took place at orchestra level in front of the proskenion façade of Ionic columns (in other similar theaters, Doric was more common). In the theater at Athens, about this time, a more monumental façade was built for the scene building, with columned wings or paraskenia projecting from its ends; later a proskenion was stretched between the paraskenia.

Ultimately the form known best from the later phase of the theater at Priene (Plate 98) became common, with the roof of the proskenion—the regular place for acting—thus opening up large sections of the wall of the scene building behind to arrange scenic effects. Later, too, the proskenion might encroach on the orchestra, and the orchestra lose its clear, distinct, circular form, as at Delos, Pergamum, and Delphi (Plate 99). This had the effect of integrating the scene and proskenion more closely to the theatron. When the orchestra was a distinct full circle the scene building was a mere external tangent to the circle, while the theatron was a natural development of the circle itself. Later, when the line of the proskenion—an element of the scene complex—cut across the perimeter of the circle of the orchestra, both scene buildings and theatron were natural developments of parts of the same circle. This closer unity, then, gave clearer integration to the several solid elements and clearer definition to the enclosed volume than in the older form, when the seats of the theatron and the structure of the scene building simply confronted each other across the circle of the orchestra.

A building of an entirely different kind that sums up in a way the aesthetic of monumental architecture in the Hellenistic period is the Great Altar at Pergamum (Plates 100, 101). The altar itself, a massive rectangular platform of a type well known since archaic times, was located on a broad platform approached by steps all along one side. The top of the platform was surrounded by rectangular piers with attached Ionic columns in front and back. Behind these, on three sides, was a wall which ran out on the projecting podia flanking the stairs. Around the outside of the wall ran Ionic columns; at the top of the stairs these columns matched the piers of the inner rectangle. Sculptures representing the titanic battle of gods and giants, on a grand scale, ran around the basement of the platform, and there were others on a slighter scale on the wall behind the piers. The effect was impressive: approaching, one would have seen the great mass of the structure looming up; one would ascend the tremendous flight of stairs between the projecting colonnaded podia, proceed through the outer columns, through the inner piers, to the inner rectangle surrounding the altar itself, which, in turn, rose conspicuously above the floor of the platform in the middle. The detail cannot be assessed completely, since much of it seems to have been left unfinished; but the exterior sculpture is used so lavishly—especially its powerful, surging movements— dramatic—even sensational—that it infuses the architectural composition with a vigor and restlessness that is new. With all its individuality, the structure is typical of the new age in greater emphasis on volume, in the relationship of separate entities of mass and volume, and in greater emphasis on movement.

Domestic architecture becomes much clearer after the fifth century. The many houses discovered at Olynthos, dating from the early part of the fourth century or a little before, reveal a type of dwelling hitherto unknown, though it may have developed,

43

somehow, from the type observed in Athens in the fifth century. In essence the house was substantially square, with an approximately square interior courtyard, along one side of which ran a wide corridor for the whole width of the house—called the pastas. Some of the rooms opened off the pastas, some off the courtyard. The entrance, too, led into the courtyard. There were second-story rooms in some parts of some houses, at least. Only one of the rooms would normally have been at all elaborate—a more or less rectangular dining room, often identified by a characteristic mosaic floor with a band, sometimes slightly raised, around three of the four sides. If there were courtyard columns supporting a roof or balcony, they were slender and often carefully made.

This type of house is known also at Delos (Plate 102, lower right) in the third and second century, but other houses at Delos (Plate 102) lacked the characteristic pastas, and seem more in the tradition of the old Athenian house. But in almost all houses of any size the court had a peristyle, and this is the significant development: the creation of an interior room open to the sky, as distinct from a yard on which the rooms of the house faced. But it is still true that the several rooms, including the peristyle, retained their rectangular simplicity and their distinctness, and were not composed as spaces developing one from the other.

The "megaron" type of house, known at Larissa in the fifth century and before, was used also in the fourth century and later at Priene (Plates 103, left, and 104). In this type the courtyard, while an integral part of the house, remained a yard on which the main building faced, but such houses were often remodeled to the peristyle form (Plate 103, right).

Finally the Hellenistic phase of Greek architecture is marked by new attitudes in the planning of groups of buildings. In a comparison, for example, of sanctuaries whose plan was defined by the end of the fifth century, such as Delphi (Plate 108), and the Acropolis at Athens (Plate 53) with later sanctuaries like that of Zeus at Priene (Plate 89) or of Asklepios at Kos (Plate 105), it is evident that in the earlier period the conscious emphasis at least was on the individual buildings oriented only to a processional way, whereas in the later there is a conscious intent to impose greater clarity on the exterior volumes and on the relationships among these and the buildings themselves. It is worth noting, however, that even in the later planned groups asymmetry and other irregularities are freely permitted—even in such nearly symmetrical designs as the agoras at Priene (Plate 89) and

Miletus (Plates 90, 91). The open areas were permitted to accumulate many various monuments organized only individually with reference to lines of traffic, and the defining stoas were seldom, if ever, so commanding as to dwarf the swarms of people going about their business, who therefore became themselves an element in the design. Moreover, in public spaces where the design comprehended an actual group of several buildings the space was rarely defined absolutely. Thus for all the organization that was imposed on the external space, and the closer integration of this with the building, there were provided elements of relief; a freedom within the order, as in the previous era, but an order which now consciously as well as tacitly linked the reality of substance to the reality of non-substance, and which recognized the form in both.

Once again the character of the style may be measured in part by the kind and extent of efforts to overcome or compromise with externally imposed limitations, as in the city of Pergamum (Plate 109). The precipitous terrain might well have discouraged any but the most determined—or romantic—designer, but by means of an imposing system of terraces the city was lavishly equipped with colonnaded agoras, sanctuaries, gymnasia—all in rectilinear forms though often with disproportionately narrow volumes. But it is deeply significant that, in spite of opportunities to form novel spatial configurations linked through various levels, all the forms remain within the types developed on less dramatic terrain. Each building remains independent—its own composition of mass and volume—directly related to the space around but not formally related to other building complexes.

Another measure of stylistic change is to be found in such efforts as were made to "modernize" older compositions—in the kind of changes that were felt necessary to adapt the old sanctuaries and cities to the new taste. The Agora at Athens (Plates 65, 110) was transformed in the second century so as to consist of two fully and clearly defined spaces; the Metroon-Bouleuterion complex was unified by a single continuous porch. But the defining structures remained independent buildings, and a sense of geometrically formed exterior volume was achieved without the geometrical scheme's absorbing the individuality of the several buildings. The two major exterior volumes were related and integrated—not as a single multidimensional spatial composition, but by the free and open movement between them provided through the specially adapted Middle Stoa. Finally, at

45

the extreme, in many ancient designs no fundamental changes were made. Even at Olympia (Plates 106, 107), where conditions were fully pliant, the design achieved more or less unconsciously by the fifth century, with the Echo Colonnade and the treasuries on the terrace to the north establishing the essential geometric dimensions, gave a form to the exterior space sufficient even for the new age.

In general, the novelty of Hellenistic architecture was to develop the form of interior—and, even more, of exterior—space, thus asserting the reality and unity of corporeal and incorporeal being. The general qualities of this broader reality were still those of "classic" Hellenism. It was, as before, ideal, clear, poised, tangible, regularly and logically structured. But now, more than before, it was felt to pervade the entire cosmic universe.

5 EPILOGUE:

Augustus to Constantinople: 31 B.C.–A.D. 330

The "classic" Greek tradition did not cease to be with the final domination of the Mediterranean world by Rome, but remained alive until the Christian Greek tradition of Byzantium emerged, and has indeed revived since. But to trace the classic Greek style through the Graeco-Roman world would require a close definition of what is "Roman" and what is "Graeco-Roman"—a task beyond the scope of this study. It becomes an element in the fully synthesized compound of Graeco-Roman culture and, though usually perceptible, it is not really separable. A "purely" Greek building, as the Roman completion of the Olympieion at Athens might be termed, is one that was designed in its essentials in Greek times; an "archaizing" building, like the great Propylaea at Eleusis, is merely imitative. In many an "original" building of the period, as at Palmyra and Baalbek, or in a multitude of smaller buildings in the towns of Greece and

47

the Mediterranean world in general, there are found innumerable formal elements of traditional Greek architecture and many of the principles of Greek design; but there are always fundamental modifications of the Greek principles and a fusion with Roman principles to create a new aesthetic system consonant with the ideals and values of the new, vastly larger, much more strictly disciplined world.

In the following plates, unless otherwise indicated, all dates refer to the period Before Christ.

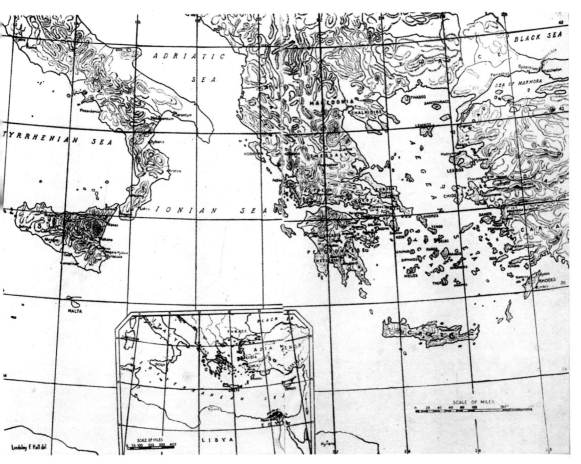

1. *Map of the Hellenic World.*

2. *The Hephaisteion, Athens, ca. 449–444. View from southwest.*

3. *The Hephaisteion. Southwest corner.*

4. *The Hephaisteion. Plan.*

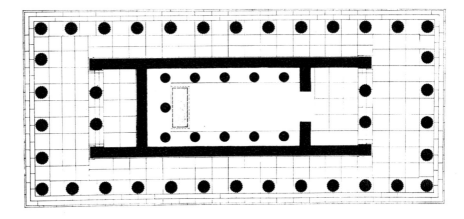

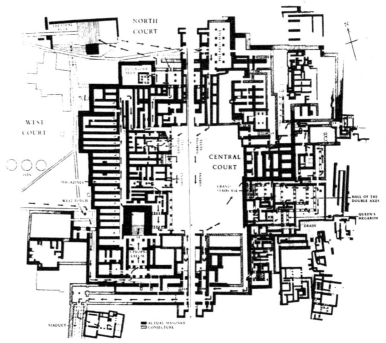

6. The Great Palace, Knossos, ca. fifteenth century. *Plan of principal levels*

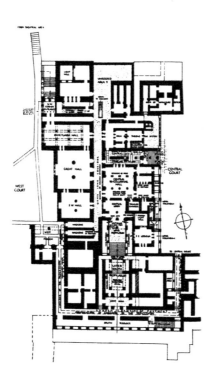

7. The Great Palace, Knossos.
"Piano Nobile." Plan.

8. *The Great Palace, Knossos. Residential apartment.*

9. *The Little Palace, Knossos, ca. fifteenth century. Plan.*

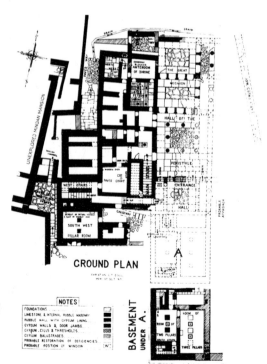

10. *The Great Palace, Knossos. The Throne Room.*

11. *Neolithic building, Tsangli in Thessaly, before 3000. Plan.*

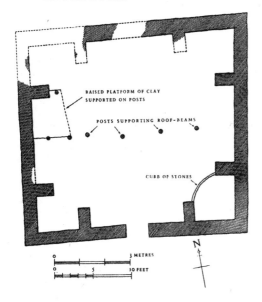

12. *The House of Tiles, Lerna, early third millennium. Plan.*

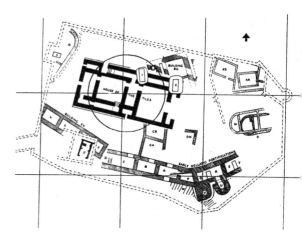

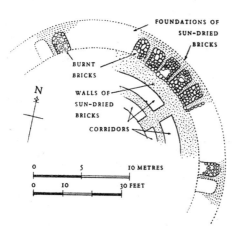

13. *Round Building, Tiryns, late third millennium. Plan.*

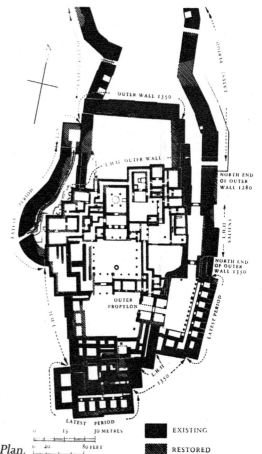

14. *Mycenaean Palace, Tiryns, ca. thirteenth century. Plan.*

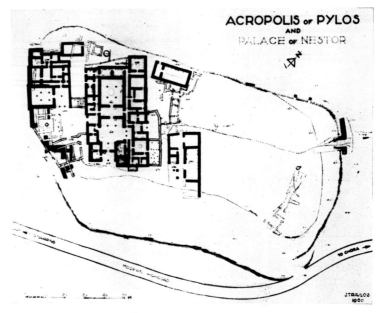

17. Mycenaean Palace, Pylos, ca. thirteenth century. Plan.

18. Octopus Vase, Minoan, 1600–1500 B.C.

19. Floor decoration in Palace, Pylos.

20. *Geometric vase, Athens, eighth century.*

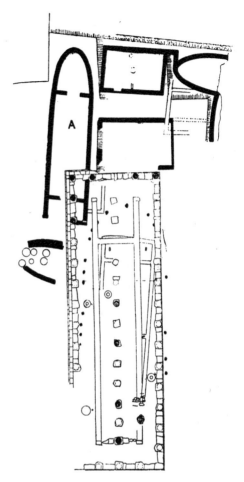

21. *Middle Helladic building, Megaron
B, and Temple of Apollo, Thermon,
second millennium, ninth century,
seventh century. Plan.*

22. Terra-cotta models of houses or temples,
Perachora and Argive Heraeum, eighth
century.

23. The Heraeum, Samos, eighth century. Plan.

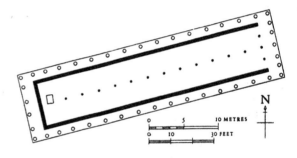

24. The Heraeum, Samos, early seventh century. Plan.

25. Temple, Naeandria, ca. 600. Plan.

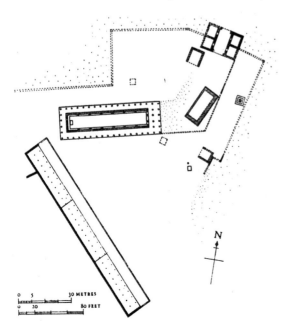

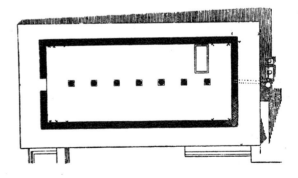

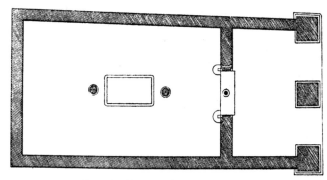

26. Temple, Prinias, Crete, seventh century. Plan.

27. Temple, Prinias. Restored view.

28. *"Aeolic Capital," Nape (Kolumdado), Mytilene, ca. 600.*

29. *Early Doric capitals, Delphi, Aegina, Corfu, ca. 600.*

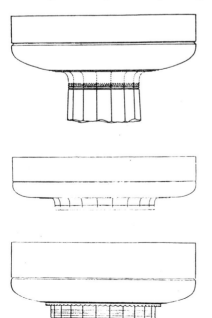

30. *Temple of Artemis, Corfu, ca. 600.*

31. *Pediment sculpture from Temple of Artemis.*

32. *Archaic Athenian vase, mid-sixth century.*   33a. *Antefix from Acropolis, Athens, sixth century.*

33b. *Treasury of Gela, Olympia. Cornice revetment, sixth century.*

34. *Archaic Temples in Magna Graecia. Plans (scale approximately 1:1000).*

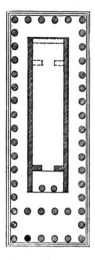

a. Zeus, Syracuse,
ca. 555.

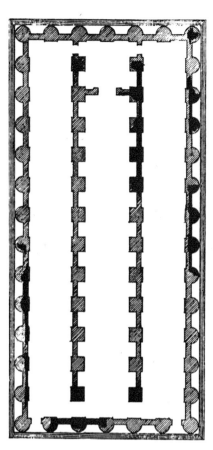

b. Zeus, Akragas, ca. 510–409.

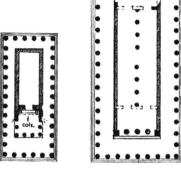

c. Athena (Ceres),   d. " Basilica,"
Paestum, ca. 510.   Paestum, ca. 53

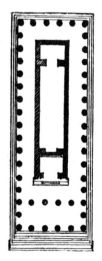

e. Selinus, "C,"
ca. 540.

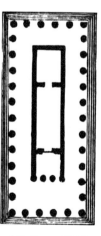

f. Selinus, "D,"
ca. 536.

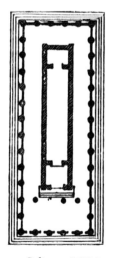

g. Selinus, " FS,"
ca. 525.

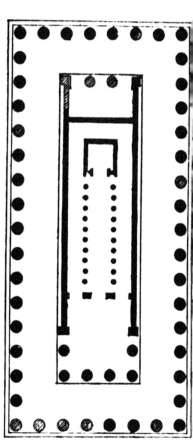

h. Selinus, "GT," ca. 520–450.

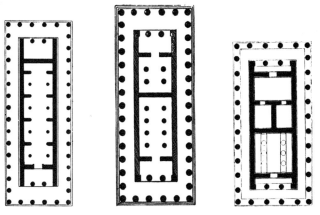

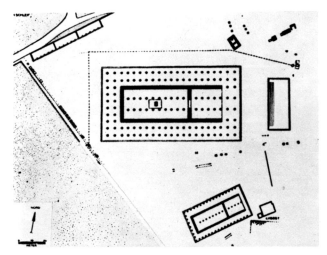

35. *Archaic temples in Greece. Plans (scale approximately 1:1000).*

a. *Hera, Olympia,* ca. *590.*   b. *Apollo, Corinth,* ca. *540.*   c. *Athena Polias, Athens,* ca. *529–515.*

36. *The Heraeum, Samos, mid-sixth century. Plan.*

38. *Temple of Apollo, Corinth, ca. 540.*

37. *The Heraeum, Olympia, sixth century. Replacement capitals.*

39. *The Temple of Athena (Ceres), Paestum, ca. 510. Reconstruction.*

40. *The Early Temple, Aegina, ca. 560. Restored entablature.*

41. *The Temple of Athena (Ceres), Paestum. Capital with necking molding.*

42. The " Basilica," Paestum, ca. 530.

43. *The Treasury of the Siphnians (as restored in the Museum), Delphi, ca. 530.*

44. *The Treasury of the Siphnians, Delphi. Moldings.*

45. *The Temple of Artemis, Ephesus, second half of the sixth century. Base of column.*

46. *The Temple of Artemis, Ephesus. Capital of column.*

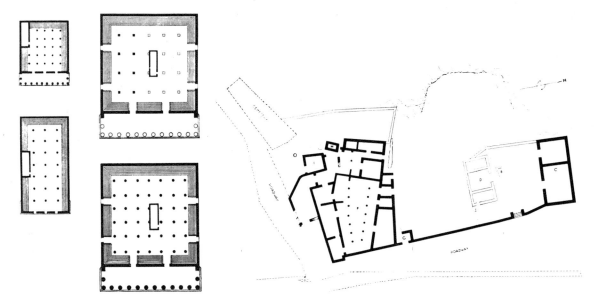

47. The Telesterion, Eleusis, stages
through sixth and fifth centuries.
Plans.

48. Council House and Prytaneion, Athens, sixth century. Plans.

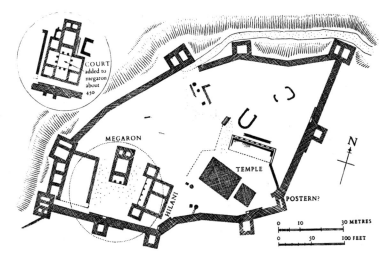

49. Houses on Acropolis, Larisa, ca. 500 and ca. 450. Plan.

50. Red-figured vase, mid-fifth century.

51. Temple of Aphaia, Aegina, ca. 490. Reconstruction.

52. *Temples in the fifth century. Plans (scale approximately 1:1000).*

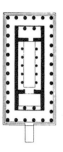

a. *Aphaia,*
Aegina,
ca. 490.

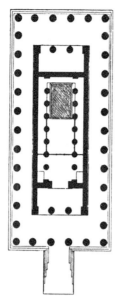

b. *Zeus, Olympia,*
ca. 468–460.

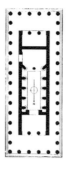

c. *Apollo, Bassae,*
450–425.

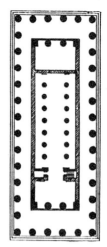

d. *Poseidon, Paestum,*
ca. 460.

53. *The Acropolis, Athens. Plan.*

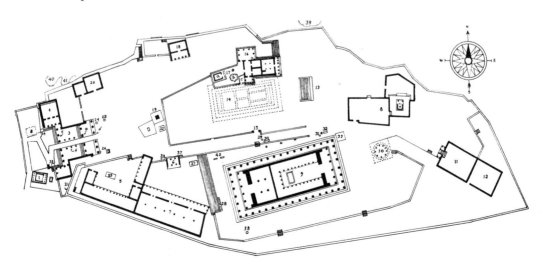

54. *The Parthenon, Athens, 447–432. General view from east.*

55. *The Parthenon, Athens. View along side, from northwest, showing curvature and entasis.*

56. *The Parthenon, Athens. Detail of corner, with entablature.*

57. The Erechtheum, Athens, ca. 421–405. View from southeast.

58. *The Erechtheum, Athens. View from northwest.*

59. The Erechtheum, Athens. Detail of moldings.

60. The Propylaea, Athens. 437–432.

61. *The Propylaea, Athens. Interior, looking eastward.*

62. *The Propylaea, Athens. Capital on interior column.*

63. *The Propylaea and Temple of Nike, Athens, as in fifth century.*

64. The Acropolis, Athens. Model.

65. The Agora, Athens, end of fifth century. Plan.

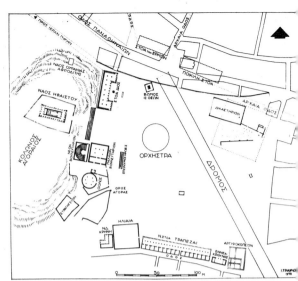

66. Stoa of Zeus, Athens, ca. 420. Plaster model.

67. Houses, Athens, fifth century. Plans

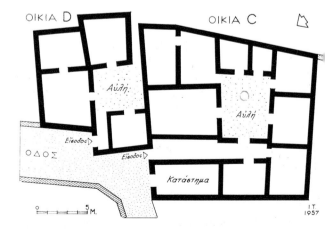

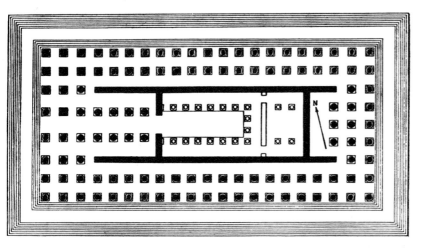

a. *Artemis, Ephesus,*
   ca. 356–236.

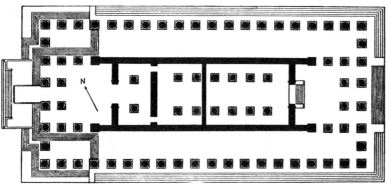

b. *Cybele, Sardis,*
   ca. 350–300.

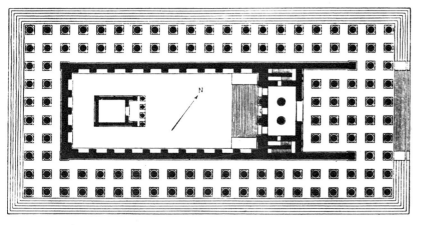

c. *Apollo, Didyma (Miletus),*
   ca. 313 B.C.–41 A.D.

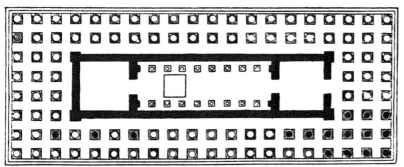

d. *Zeus Olympios, Athens,*
   ca. 174 B.C.–140 A.D.

68. Colossal Hellenistic Temples. Plans (scale approximately 1:1000).

69. Smaller Hellenistic Temples. Plans (scale approximately 1:1000).

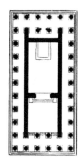
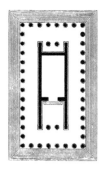
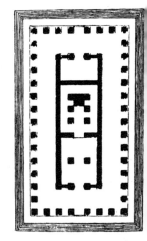

a. Athena Polias, Priene,   b. Apollo, Sminthe,
ca. 340–156.   ca. 250.

c. Artemis, Magnesia, ca. 175.

70. Temple of Artemis, Ephesus, ca. 350. Restoration.

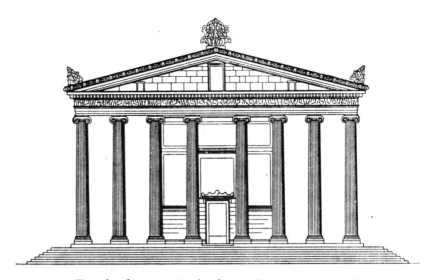

71. Temple of Artemis Leukophryne, Magnesia, ca. 175. Restoration.

72. Propylon of Sanctuary of Athena Polias, Pergamum, third century. Reconstruction.

73. Corinthian capital from Tholos, Delphi, ca. 400.

74. Corinthian capital of Temple of Athena, Tegea, ca. 350.

75. Corinthian capital of Tholos, Epidaurus, ca. 350. Elevation of restoration.

76. Corinthian capital of Monument of Lysikrates, Athens, ca. 334.

77. Corinthian columns of Olympieion, Athens, ca. 170.

78. *Moldings from Temple of Athena, Tegea, ca. 350.*

79. *Moldings from Tholos, Epidaurus, ca. 350.*

80. Base of Column from Temple of Apollo, Didyma (Miletus), Hellenistic period.

81. Capital from Temple of Apollo, Didyma.

82. The South Stoa, Corinth, ca. 325. Plan and elevation.

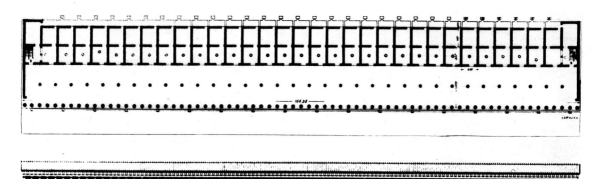

83. The South Stoa, Corinth. Reconstruction of end.

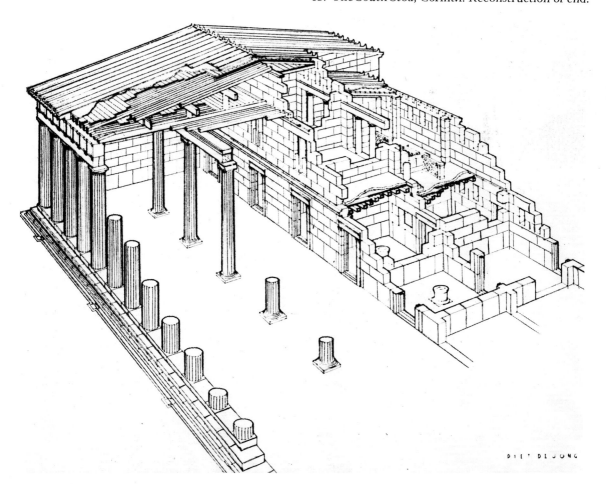

DIE' DEJONG

84. *The Stoa of Attalos, Athens, ca. 150. Sectional model.*

85. *The Stoa of Attalos, Athens. View from exterior, as rebuilt.*

86. *The Stoa of Attalos, Athens. Interior, into first floor, as rebuilt.*

87. *The Stoa of Attalos, Athens. Interior, first floor, as rebuilt.*

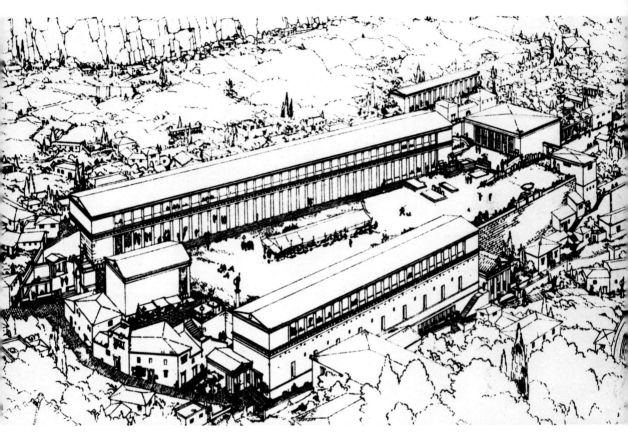

88. The Agora, Assos, ca. third century. Reconstruction.

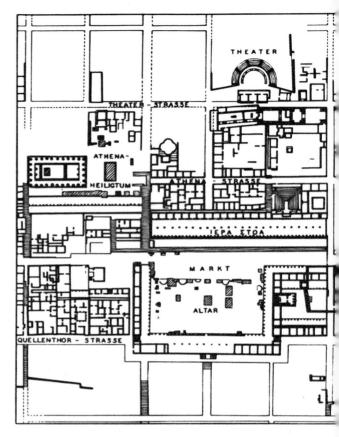

89. The Agora and environs, Priene, fourth century. Plan

90. The Area of the Agoras, Miletus, fourth century. Plan.

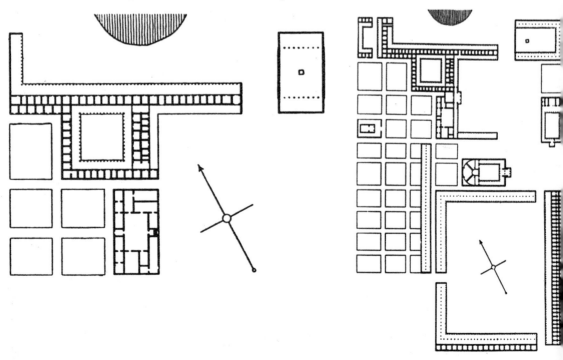

91. The Area of the Agoras, Miletus,
second century. Plan.

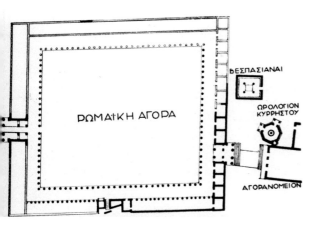

ΘΕΣΠΑΣΙΑΝΑΙ

ΩΡΟΛΟΓΙΟΝ
ΚΥΡΡΗΣΤΟΥ

ΡΩΜΑΪΚΗ ΑΓΟΡΑ

ΑΓΟΡΑΝΟΜΕΙΟΝ

92. *The Roman Market, Athens, first century. Plan.*

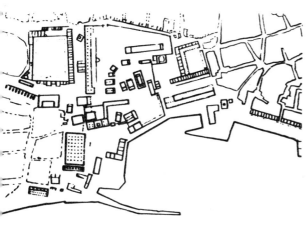

93. *Sanctuary and Agoras, Delos, ca. second century. Plan.*

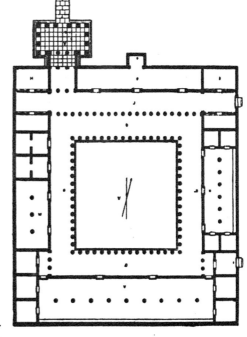

94. *The Palaestra, Epidaurus, third century. Plan.*

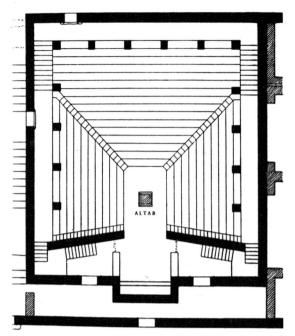

95. The Ekklesiasterion, Priene, ca. 200. Plan.

96. The Ekklesiasterion, Priene. View of interior. Restored.

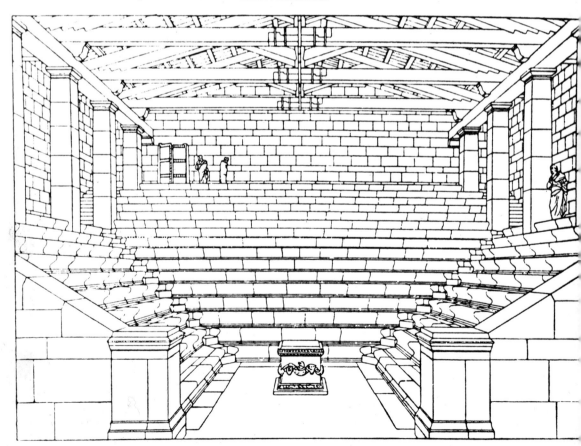

98. The Theater, Priene, third century. Restoration.

99. The Theater, Delphi, second century.

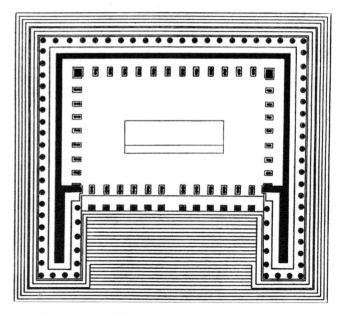

100. *The Great Altar of Zeus, Pergamum, second century. Plan.*

101. *The Great Altar of Zeus, Pergamum, As rebuilt.*

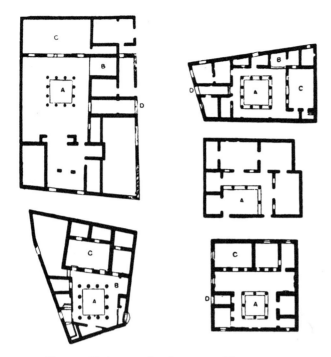

102. *Houses, Delos, ca. third century. Plans.*

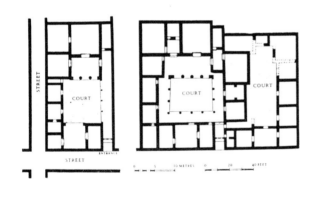

103. *House, Priene, fourth century. Plan.*

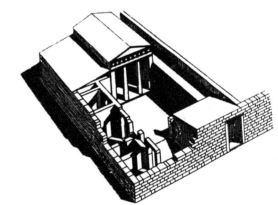

104. *House, Priene. Restored view.*

105. *Sanctuary of Asklepios, Kos, ca. second century. Restoration.*

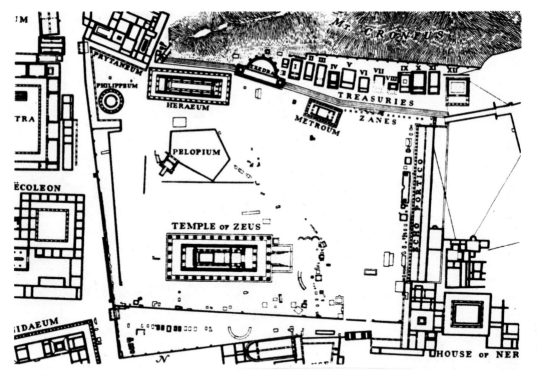

106. *Sanctuary of Zeus, Olympia. Plan.*

107. *Sanctuary of Zeus, Olympia. Restored view.*

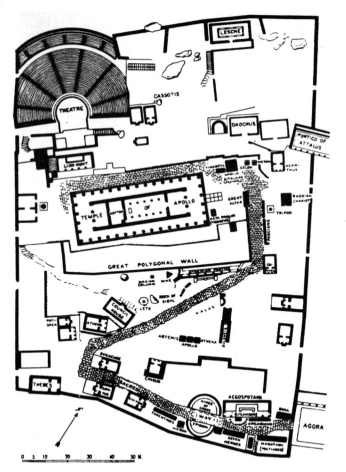

Within the Delphi plan, the following labels appear:

LESCHE

THEATRE

CASSOTIS

DAOCHUS

PORTICO OF ATTALUS

ACANTHUS

LION HUNT

TIMASITHEA

APOLLO

ATTALUS

CLEOBIS

HIERON

GREAT ALTAR

RHODIAN CHARIOT

TRIPOD

TEMPLE OF APOLLO

ACH. PRINS (PERSEUS)

GREAT POLYGONAL WALL

NAXIAN COLUMN

NIKE

ROCK OF SIBYL

LETO

COUNCIL HOUSE

PORTI DACA

ATHENS

HALOS

DIONYSUS

ARTEMIS ATHENA

APOLLO

SYRACUSE

CNIDUS

THEBES

SACRED

TARENTINES

HIERON

KINGS OF ARGOS

LYSANDER

WAY

MARATHON (MILTIADES)

SEVEN HEROES

AEGOSPOTAMI

ARCADIANS

BULL

AGORA

0 5 10   20   30   40   50 M.

108. Sanctuary of Apollo, Delphi. Plan.

Within the Pergamum plan, the following labels appear:

STORE-HOUSES

BARRACKS

CARACALLA TEMPLE

TRAJANEUM

PALACE

LIBRARY

THEATRE

ATHENA TEMPLE

GATEWAY

ALTAR

HEROON

AGORA

N
W   E
S

109. The Upper City, Pergamum. Plan.

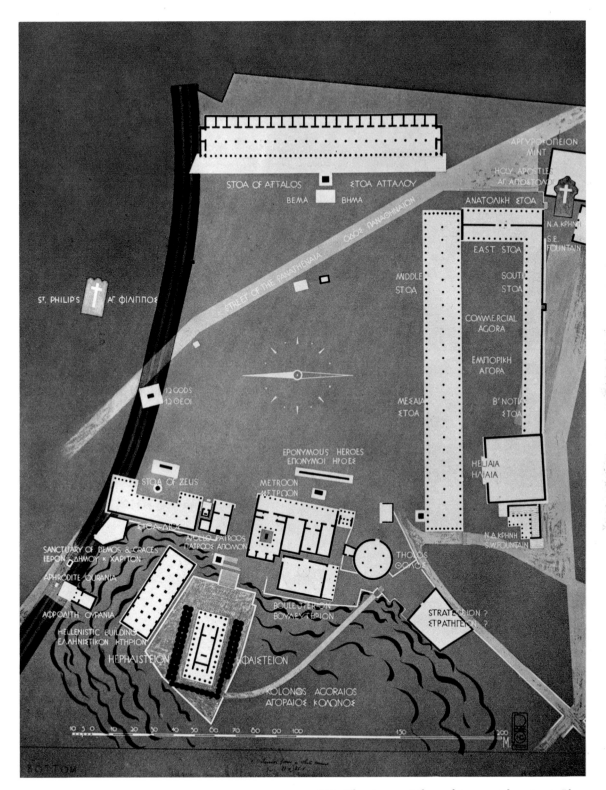

Within the image, the following labels appear:

STOA OF ATTALOS   ΣΤΟΑ ΑΤΤΑΛΟΥ
BEMA   BHMA

ΑΡΓΥΡΟΚΟΠΕΙΟΝ
MINT
HOLY APOSTLES
ΑΓ. ΑΠΟΣΤΟΛΟΙ
ΑΝΑΤΟΛΙΚΗ ΣΤΟΑ
N.A. KPHNH
S.E. FOUNTAIN

EAST STOA
MIDDLE STOA   SOUTH STOA
ST. PHILIP'S   ΑΓ ΦΙΛΙΠΠΟΣ
STREET OF THE PANATHENAIA   ΟΔΟΣ ΠΑΝΑΘΗΝΑΙΟΝ
COMMERCIAL AGORA
ΕΜΠΟΡΙΚΗ ΑΓΟΡΑ
12 GODS   12 ΘΕΟΙ
ΜΕΣΑΙΑ ΣΤΟΑ   B΄ ΝΟΤΙΑ ΣΤΟΑ
EPONYMOUS HEROES   ΕΠΟΝΥΜΟΙ ΗΡΟΕΣ
HELIAIA   ΗΛΙΑΙΑ
STOA OF ZEUS   METROON   ΜΕΤΡΩΟΝ
ΣΤΟΑ ΔΙΟΣ   APOLLO PATROOS   ΠΑΤΡΟΟΣ ΑΠΟΛΟΩΝ
SANCTUARY OF DEMOS & GRACES   N.A. KPHNH S.W. FOUNTAIN
ΙΕΡΟΝ ΔΗΜΟΥ Κ ΧΑΡΙΤΟΝ
APHRODITE OURANIA   THOLOS   ΘΟΛΟΣ
ΑΦΡΟΔΙΤΗ ΟΥΡΑΝΙΑ   STRATEGION ?   ΣΤΡΑΤΗΓΕΙΟΝ ?
BOULEUTERION   ΒΟΥΛΕΥΤΗΡΙΟΝ
HELLENISTIC BUILDING
ΕΛΛΗΝΙΣΤΙΚΟΝ ΚΤΗΡΙΟΝ
HEPHAISTEION   ΗΦΑΙΣΤΕΙΟΝ
KOLONOS AGORAIOS
ΑΓΟΡΑΙΟΣ ΚΟΛΟΝΟΣ

110. *The Agora, Athens, late second century. Plan.*

111. *The Portland Vase, first century.*

NOTES

Information on most of the buildings mentioned in the text, and on other related buildings, and on other kinds of monuments, may be found readily in and through the works of Dinsmoor, Lawrence, and Robertson cited in the bibliography. In the following notes are references to some significant material published since Lawrence's book.

1. Strictly speaking the building has only three steps, but the top of the foundation, although of limestone rather than marble, is clearly visible and presents essentially the appearance and serves the function of a step. It should be noted also that in the plan (Plate 4) the interior colonnade is shown as having three columns across the back; although there is a tendency to think that there should be four, this plan is used here because of its completeness and clarity.

2. The relatively great importance of the builder as compared with the designer is perhaps overemphasized by Bundgaard (*Mnesicles*, esp. pp. 93-99), but the principle is probably sound.

3. On the functional aspect of Minoan palaces, see also recent articles by J. Walter Graham in *American Journal of Archaeology*, LX (1956), pp. 151-57; LXI (1957), pp. 255-62; LXIII (1959), pp. 47-52; LXIV (1960), pp 329-33 and 335-41; LXV (1961), pp. 165-72; and *idem, The Palaces of Crete* (Princeton, 1962).

4. On the House of the Tiles and other buildings at Lerna, see J. L. Caskey, *Hesperia*, XXIII (1954), pp. 3-30, esp. 23-27; XXIV (1955), pp. 25-49, esp. 37-41; XXV (1956), pp. 146-73, esp. 162-69; XXVI (1957), pp. 142-62; XXVII (1958), pp. 125-44, esp. 127-29; XXVIII (1959), pp. 202-7.

5. For a Mycenaean private house see Nicholas Verdelis, *Archaeology*, XIV (1961), pp. 12-17.

6. See George Mylonas, *Mycenae*, pp. 103-76.

7. For the Palace at Pylos see C. W. Blegen, *American Journal of Archaeology*, LX (1956), pp. 95-101; LXI (1957), pp. 129-35; LXIII (1959), pp. 121-27; LXIV (1960), pp. 153-60; LXV (1961), pp. 153-58.

8. Compare Dinsmoor, *Architecture of Ancient Greece*, pp. 40-41. On the origin of the peripteral colonnade there is an intriguing possibility exactly contrary to the relatively conventional suggestion in the text. At Olympia in Roman times there was a structure of four columns supporting a roof protecting an ancient wooden pillar said to have belonged to the house of Oenomaos, and other columns supporting a roof over the tomb of Oxylus (*Pausanias*, V, 20, 6; VI, 24, 9), (Dinsmoor, p. 53; Robertson, p. 66). Other "monopteral" buildings—colonnades without walls—are known (cf. Dinsmoor, p. 116, n.3), and especially one at Samos (Hans Schleif, *Mitteilungen des Deutschen Archäologischen Instituts, Athenische Abteilung*, LVIII (1933), pp. 211 ff., esp. pp. 212-17) built apparently to protect the image during a reconstruction of the great temple in the sixth century. Is it possible that the peripteral form evolved actually from a kind of monopteral structure—a "baldacchino"—of the period around the tenth century?

9. Plate 36 shows the sanctuary of Hera at Samos as projected in the early part of the sixth century under the architect Rhoikos. The great temple was barely begun when a fire compelled a new start around the middle of the century; the new version, of the tyrant Polykrates, had three rows of columns front and back, stood on a high platform, and had other peculiarities. It is conveniently illustrated by Lawrence (p. 136, Fig. 77). One might note in our plan the South Building, notable for the single row of columns on axis characteristic of early temples, combined with the broader proportion and almost pseudodipteral colonnade. For the early buildings at Samos see *Mitteilungen des Deutschen Archäologischen Instituts, Athenische Abteilung,* LV (1930), pp. 1-99; LVIII (1933), pp. 146-247; LXXII (1957), pp. 52-151.–the later articles presenting some corrections of details of restoration in the earlier.

10. We have ignored the intricate and problematic history of the predecessors of the Periclean Parthenon, and the related problems of the history of the Old Athena Temple. The most recent "general theory" is Dinsmoor's incorporated in his *Architecture of Ancient Greece;* some differences in interpretation are argued by W. H. Plommer in the *Journal of Hellenic Studies,* LXXX (1960), pp. 127-59.

11. See Dinsmoor, pp. 199-205; also Bundgaard, J. A., *Mnesicles.*

12. For a smaller sixth-century replacement of this seventh-century stoa, built in the sixth century, see Plate 36.

13. G. P. Stevens, *The Periclean Entrance Court of the Acropolis of Athens* (New York, 1936) pp. 17-28.

14. H. A. Thompson, *Hesperia,* XXIII (1954), pp. 39-45.

15. For examples of this type of building see Dinsmoor (pp. 322, 329) and Lawrence (pp. 219-21, Fig. 123; p. 249).

16. Oscar Broneer, "The South Stoa and its Roman Successors," *Corinth, Results of Excavations conducted by the American School of Classical Studies at Athens,* Vol. 1, Pt. 4 (Princeton, 1954), esp. pp. 18-99.

17. H. A. Thompson, "The Stoa of Attalos II in Athens," *Picture Book* No. 2, *American School of Classical Studies at Athens* (Princeton, 1959).

18. John Travlos, *Poleodomike Exelexis ton Athenon,* pp. 100-2.

GLOSSARY

abacus   the plaque constituting the topmost element of a capital, on which the architrave rests

adyton   a secluded room, often one behind the cella of a temple

akroterion   an ornamental device at the peak or corners of a gable

antefix   the ornamental end of a cover-tile in a roofing system

architrave   the beam lying across the columns

arris   the edge between two planes, especially between the flutes of a Doric column

cella   the main enclosed room of a temple, or a temple or temple-like building without surrounding columns

dromos   a "road," usually the partially sunken passage leading into an underground tomb

echinus   the curved, cushion-like element in a Doric or sometimes Ionic capital making the transition from the shaft of the
column to the abacus

entablature   the parts of a façade above the columns, or sometimes only the architrave, frieze, and cornice but not the
gables

entasis   the curve in the vertical profile of a column

fascia   a narrow band, or broad fillet, usually one of three such
surfaces running horizontally on an Ionic architrave

gutta   a "drop," suggesting the head of a peg or nail, under the
regula or mutule in a Doric entablature

hypostyle   characterized by columns distributed fairly evenly
throughout a space to support the ceiling

metope   a rectangular surface, sometimes smooth, sometimes
sculptured, in the frieze of a Doric entablature

mutule   a rectangular plaque on the under surface of a Doric
cornice, ornamented with rows of guttae

naos   a temple, or often the part of a temple enclosed by walls;
roughly, the Greek equivalent of "cella"

odeion   a music hall

palmette   an ornament suggesting a hand displayed flat and
erect, or perhaps the fronds of a palm tree

paraskenion   the projecting structure at each end of a proskenion in a Greek theater

pediment   a gable, or triangular element rimmed by cornices at
the top of a façade

peripteral   characterized by being surrounded on the exterior
by columns

peripteron   the colonnade surrounding a peripteral building;
usually refers to the columns themselves but sometimes also
to the space between columns and wall

peristyle   a colonnade surrounding an open space, usually
within a room or a court within a building, (but sometimes
used also as synonym of "peripteron" or "peripteral")

podium a platform of distinct elevation supporting a building

pronaos the porch in front of a naos formed by the forward projection of the side walls

propylaea a complex propylon

propylon a gate building

proskenion a one-story façade with a narrow roof running along the front of the skene (see below) in a Greek theater

prytaneion the headquarters of the prytanies, or presiding officers of an administration

regula a narrow, rectangular batten-like element at the top of a Doric architrave below the taenia and triglyph

scene building the structure behind the orchestra in a Greek theater

sima the raised barrier at the lower edge of a roof diverting rain water to specified outlets

skene the principal, original part of the scene building, for storage, dressing rooms, and as "back-drop" for the action

stylobate the course of stone on which columns rest

taenia the top of an architrave, above both the beam and the regula, but below the triglyph.

tholos a circular building

triglyph a slightly projecting rectangular element in a Doric frieze characterized by two vertical beveled cuttings and correspondingly beveled corners

volute a scroll- or ribbon-like motif terminating in a spiral

BIBLIOGRAPHY

Three books provide all that could be expected as an introduction to the facts of the history of Greek architecture, and through their bibliographies direct the student easily to sources and larger treatments of all problems:

DINSMOOR, W. B., *Architecture of Ancient Greece*. 3rd ed. of Anderson, Spiers, Dinsmoor, London and New York, Batsford, 1950, with 40 pages of closely analyzed bibliography.

LAWRENCE, A. W., *Greek Architecture*. London, Penguin, 1957, with biliographies for each chapter—mostly according to periods. This is especially important for the Minoan-Mycenaean material.

ROBERTSON, D. S., *Greek and Roman Architecture*. 2nd ed., New York, Cambridge University Press, 1945. With chronological lists of buildings and thirty pages of bibliography, mostly topographical.

Recent works on Greek architecture as such, and others with special pertinence:

BUNDGAARD, J. A., *Mnesicles.* Copenhagen, Gyldendal, 1957.

CALI, FRANÇOIS, *L'Ordre Grec*, photographies de Serge Moulinier. Paris, Arthaud, 1958.

DURM, J., *Die Baukunst der Griechen. Handbuch der Architektur*, II, 1. 3rd ed., Leipzig, 1910.

FYFE, T., *Hellenistic Architecture.* New York, Cambridge University Press, 1936.

HODGE, A. T., *The Woodwork of Greek Roofs.* New York, Cambridge University Press, 1960.

KRAUSS, F., *Paestum.* Berlin, Mann, 1943.

———, *Die Tempel von Paestum.* Erster Teil, *Der Athenatempel und die sogenannte Basilika.* 1. Lieferung, *Der Athenatempel.* Deutsches Archäologisches Institut, *Denkmäler Antiker Architektur*, Band 9/1. Berlin, deGruyter, 1959.

KRIESIS, A., "Ancient Greek Town Building," *Acta Congressus Madvigiani*, 1954, Vol. IV. Copenhagen, 1958, pp. 27-86.

LEHMANN, P., "The Setting of Hellenistic Temples," *Journal of the Society of Architectural Historians*, XIII, 1954, pp. 15-20.

MARTIN, R., *Recherches sur l'Agora Grecque.* Paris, Boccard, 1951.

REUTHER, O., *Der Heratempel von Samos.—Der Bau seit der Zeit des Polykrates.* Berlin, Mann, 1957.

SCRANTON, R., "Interior Design of Greek Temples," *American Journal of Archaeology*, L, 1946, pp. 39-51.

———, "Group Design in Greek Architecture," *Art Bulletin*, XXXI, 1949, pp. 247-68.

STEVENS, G. P., "Architecture," *in* Fowler, H. N., and Wheeler, J. R., *Handbook of Greek Archaeology.* New York, American Book Company, 1909.

STILLWELL, R., "The Siting of Classical Greek Temples," *Journal of the Society of Architectural Historians*, XIII, 1954, pp. 3-8.

THOMPSON, H. A., "The Agora at Athens and the Greek Market Place," *Journal of the SAH*, XIII, 1954, pp. 9-14.

TRAVLOS, J., *Poleodomike Exelexis ton Athenon.* Athens, Konstantinides and Michales, 1960.

WYCHERLEY, R. E., *How the Greeks Built Cities.* New York, Macmillan, 1949.

Some recent and other pertinent works on related matters:

BIEBER, M., *The Sculpture of the Hellenistic Age*. New York, Columbia University Press, 1955.

BONNARD, ANDRÉ, *Greek Civilization*. New York, Macmillan, 1959.

BOTSFORD-ROBINSON, *Hellenic History*. 4th ed., New York, Macmillan, 1956.

BOWRA, C. M., *Greek Experience*. London, Weidenfield and Nicolson, 1957.

COOK, R. M., *Greek Painted Pottery*. Chicago, Ill., Quadrangle; London, Methuen, 1960.

CARPENTER, R., *Esthetic Basis of Greek Art*. 2nd ed., Bloomington, Ind., Indiana University Press, 1959.

———, *Greek Sculpture*. Chicago, Ill., Chicago University Press, 1960.

HILL, I. T., *Ancient City of Athens*. London, Methuen, 1953.

MARINATOS, S., and HIRMER, M., *Crete and Mycenae*. New York, Abrams, 1960.

MATZ, F., *Geschichte der Griechischen Kunst. I. Die Geometrische und die Früharchaische Form*. Frankfurt a.M., Klostermann, 1950.

MYLONAS, G., *Ancient Mycenae*. Princeton, N.J., Princeton University Press, 1957.

RICHTER, G. M. A., *A Handbook of Greek Art*. London, Phaidon, 1959.

———, *Sculpture and Sculptors of the Greeks*. 2nd ed., New Haven, Conn., Yale University Press, 1950.

RODENWALDT, G., *Die Kunst der Antike (Hellas und Rom). Propyläen Kunstgeschichte*, III. Berlin, 1927.

ROSTOVTZEFF, M., *A History of the Ancient World*. New York, Oxford University Press, 1926.

SCHODER, R. V., *Masterpieces of Greek Art*. Greenwich, Conn., New York Graphic, 1960.

STARR, C. G., *The Origins of Greek Civilization*. New York, Knopf, 1961.

TARN, W. W., *Hellenistic Civilization*. London, Arnold, 1952.

WACE, A. J. B., *Mycenae*. Princeton, N.J., Princeton University Press, 1949.

121

INDEX

Numbers in regular roman type refer to text pages; *italic* figures refer to the plates.

Acropolis, the (Athens) 30, 32, 34, 44, *53*, *64*; antefix from, *33a*; fortifications of, 29
Aegean Islands architecture of, 21, 26
Aegina, 29; early Doric capitals, *29*; Early Temple, 29, *40*; Temple of Aphaia, 29, *51*, *52d*
"Aeolic" style, 25, 26, *28*
Agora, 35, 44–5, Assos, 40, *88*; Athens, 32–33, 40, 45, *65*, *110*; Corinth, 39, *82*, *83*; Delos, 41–42, *93*; Miletus, 44–45, *90*, *91*; Priene, 44–45, *89*
Akragas, Temple of Concord, 30; Temple of Zeus, *34b*
Altar of Zeus, Great, Pergamum, 43, *100*, *101*
Archaic buildings, 24–5, 26, 28; *see also* Archaic Temples
Archaic Athenian vase, *32*
Archaic Temples in Magna Graecia, 26–29, 30, *34a–h*
Argive Heraeum, 21, 34, *22*
Artemesium, Magnesia, 38, *69c*, *71*
Asia Minor, 21, 24, 25, 26, 29, 40; *see also* Larisa, Miletus, Priene
Assembly hall, 42, Eleusis, 33–34, *47*; *see also* Ekklesiasterion and Bouleuterion
Assos, 40, *88*
Atreus, Treasury of, Mycenae, *16*

Athens, Acropolis, 29, 30, 32, 34, 44, 33a, 53, 64; Agora, 32–33, 40, 45, 65, 110; archaic vase, 32; Choregic Monument of Lysikrates, 39, 76; Council House and Prytaneion, 33, 34, 48, 65; Erechtheum, 31, 32, 57, 58, 59; geometric vase, 20; Hephaisteion, 9, 11, 12, 24, 25, 29, 30, 32, 2, 3, 4, 5; houses in, 67; Odeion of Pericles, 34; Olympieion, 39, 47, 77; Parthenon, 30–31, 53, 54, 55, 56, 64; Propylaea, 31–32, 53, 60, 61, 62, 63; Roman Market, 40, 41, 92; Sanctuary of Artemis of Brauron, 32, 53, 64; Stoa of Attalos, 40, 84, 85, 86, 87; Stoa of Zeus, 32–33, 66; Temple of Athena Nike, 32, 63; Temple of Zeus Olympios, 68d; Theater, 42

Bases of columns, 39, 45, 63, 80
"Basilica," Delos, 41–42, 93
"Basilica," Paestum, 34d, 42
Bassae, 39; Temple of Apollo, 52c
Bouleuterion, Miletus, 42, 91
Building materials; in "classic" period, 10; in Early Helladic period, 17–18; about eighth century, 21; in fifth century, 32–33; in fourth century, 39; of Minoan architecture, 16; in Middle Helladic period, 20; in Neolithic period, 15; in seventh century, 24–25, 33a, b; in sixth century, 26; in Temple of Artemis, Garitsa, 25–26, 30
Byzantium, 47

Capitals, 38–39; Aeolic, 25, 26, 28; Choregic Monument of Lysikrates, 39, 76; Doric, 27, 29, 37, 41; Heraeum, Olympia, 37; Ionic, 25, 27, 39, 46; Olympieion, Athens, 39, 77; Propylea, Athens, 32, 62; Temple of Apollo, Didyma, 81; Temple of Athena, Tegea, 74; Temple of Athena (Ceres), Paestum, 41; Temple of Artemis, Ephesus, 46; Tholos, Delphi, 39, 73; Tholos, Epidaurus, 75
Cecrops, Tomb of, 31
Cella, 9, 24; see also Naos, Temples
Ceramics, 21
Chamber tombs, 19; see also Tombs
Choregic Monument of Lysikrates, 39, 76
Civic buildings, 33–34, 48
"Classic" design, 9–13, 20–21, 23–35, 47
Corfu (Kerkyra, Corcyra), 25; Early Doric capitals, 29; Temple of Artemis, 25–26, 30, 31
Corinth, 29, 39; South Stoa, 39, 82, 83; Temple of Apollo, 29, 35b, 38
Corinthian capital, 38–39; Monument of Lysikrates, Athens, 76; Temple of Athena, Tegea, 74; Tholos, Delphi, 73; Tholos, Epidaurus, 75
Corinthian columns of Olympieion, Athens, 39, 47, 77
Council House, Olympia, 33
Council House, Athens, 33, 34, 48, 65
Crete, 14–15, 18, 19, 21, 26; Temple, Prinias, 26, 26, 27, see also Knossos, Minoan

Delos, 41–42, 44; houses at, 102; Sanctuary and Agoras, 93; Theater at, 42, 99
Delphi, 25, 29, 32, 34, 39, 42, 44; Corinthian capital from Tholos, 73; early Doric capitals, 29; Marmaria, 25, 39; Sanctuary of Apollo, 44, 108; Theater at, 42, 99; Treasury of the Siphnians, 29, 43, 44
Domestic architecture, 15–19, 24, 34, 43–44, 67; at Delos, 44, 102; Early Helladic, 17–18; in Great Palace, Knossos, 8; on the Acropolis, Larisa, 49; of Argive Heraeum, 22; at Perachora, 22; at Olynthos, 43; House of Tiles at Lerna, 18, 12; Late Helladic, 18–19; "megaron" type at Larisa, 44; Minoan, 15–17
Doric order, 11, 21, 25, 27, 28–29, 38, 39, 42, 29, 30, 39, 40

Echo Colonnade, Olympia, 46
Ekklesiasterion, Priene, 42, 95, 96
Eleusis, 34, 47; Propylea, 47; Shrine of Demeter (Telesterion), 33–34, 47

Ephesus, 38; Temple of Artemis, *45, 46, 68a, 70*
Epidaurus, 39, 42; Palaestra, 41, *94*; Theater, 42, *97*; Tholos, 39, *75, 79*
Erechtheum, Athens, 31, 32, *53, 57, 58, 59, 64*

Floor decoration, *19*
Fortifications, 19, 29
Frieze, 25, 28, 38; Hephaisteion, 10, 11; Parthenon, 30

Garitsa, Temple of Artemis, 25–26, *30, 31*
Gela, Treasury of, Olympia, 25, *33b*
Geometric style, 21, *20*
Great Altar of Zeus, Pergamum, 43, *100, 101*
Great Palace, the, Knossos, see Knossos
Gymnasium, 37, 41, 45, *94*; see also Palaestra

Hagia Triada, 15
Helladic architecture: Early period, 17–18, 19; Middle period, 18, 19, 20; Late period, 18–20
Hellenic World, map of, *1*
Hellenistic Temples, colossal, *68a–d*; smaller, *69a–c*
Hephaisteion, Athens, 9, 11, 12, 24, 25, 29, 30, 32, *2, 3, 5*; plan of, *4*
Hera Basileia, Pergamum, 38
Heraeum, Olympia, 25, *35a*, 37
Heraeum, Samos; first, 21, 32, *23*; second, 25, 32, *24*; third, 27, *36*; fourth, 27, 38
Hesiod, 23, 24
Hippodameian system of town planning, 35
Homer, 23
House of Tiles, Lerna, 18, *12*
"Hypostyle Hall," Delos, 41–42, *93*

Ionic order, 25, 27, 29, 31, 32, 39, 42, 43, *41, 45, 46*

Knossos, 15–17, 20; Great Palace of, 15, 16, 17, *6, 7, 8, 10*; Little Palace of, *9*
Kolumdado (Nape), Mytilene, 25, 26, *28*
Kos, Sanctuary of Asklepios, 44, *105*

Larisa, 26, 34, 44; houses on Acropolis, *49*
Lerna, House of Tiles, 18, *12*
Linear form, 16–17, 25
Lion Gate, at Palace, Mycenae, 20, *15*
Little Palace, Knossos, *9*
Lysikrates, Monument of, 39, *76*

Magna Graecia, 26, 28, 29, 30, 35, *34, 39, 41, 42, 52*
Magnesia, 38; Temple of Artemis, *69c*; Temple of Artemis Leukophryne, *71*
Mallia, 15
Map of Hellenic World, *1*
Marmaria, Delphi, 25, 39, *29*
Megalopolis, Thersilion, 41
Megarons, 19–20, 34, 44; Megaron B, Thermon, 21–22, 26, *21*
Messa, Temple at, 38
Metroon-Bouleuterion complex, Athens, 45
Miletus, 38, 40, 42, 45; area of the Agoras, 44–45, *90, 91*; Bouleuterion, 42, *91*; Temple
    of Apollo, 38, *68c, 80, 81*
Minoan architecture, 15–17, 20; Octopus vase, *18*, see also Knossos

Moldings, 10, 11, 27, 39, *41*; Erechtheum, Athens, 32, *59*; Temple of Athena, Tegea, 28, *78*; Tholos, Epidaurus, *79*; Treasury of the Siphnians, Delphi, *44*

Monument of Lysikrates, Athens, 39, *76*

Mycenae, 19, 20, 21, 22, 34; Lion Gate, 20, *15*; Palace at Pylos, *17*, *19*; Palace at Tiryns 20, *14*; Shaft Graves at, 18; Treasury of Atreus, 19, *16*

Mytilene, "Aeolic" capital, Nape (Kolumdado), 25, 26, *28*

Naendria, 26; Temple plan, *25*

Naos, 9, 10, 11, 13, 22, 25, 26, 27, 30, 34, 38; *see also* Cella, Temples

Nape (Kolumdado), Mytilene, 25, 26, *28*

Neolithic buildings, 14–15, 20, *11*

Odeion of Pericles, Athens, 34

Olympia, 25, 29, 33, 46; Heraeum, *37*; Sanctuary of Zeus, 46, *52*, *106*, *107*; Temple of Hera, *35a*; Treasury of Gela, 25, *33b*

Olympieion, Athens, 39, 47, 77

Olynthos, architecture of, 43–44

Paestum, 28, 30; "Basilica," *34d*, *42*; Temple of Athena (Ceres), *34c*, *39*, *41*; Temple of Poseidon, *52d*

Palaces, 15–20, *6*, *7*, *8*, *9*, *10*, *14*, *17*, *19*

Palaestra, 37; at Epidaurus, 41, *94*

Parthenon, Athens, 30–31, *53*, *54*, *55*, *56*, *64*

Pediment sculpture, Temple of Artemis, Corfu, 26, *31*

Perachora, 21, 34; houses or temples at, *22*

Pergamum, 38, 42, 43, 45, *109*; Great Altar of Zeus, 43, *100*, *101*; Sanctuary of Athena Polias, 38, *72*; Theater at, 42, *99*

Pericles, Odeion of, Athens, 34

Persian wars, 24, 29

Phaistos, 15

Plato, 23, 24

Portland Vase, *111*

Priene, 40, 42, 44, 45; Agora and environs, 45, *89*; Ekklesiasterion, 42, *95*, *96*; houses at, *103*, *104*; Sanctuary of Zeus, 44, *89*; Temple of Athena Polias, *69a*; Theater at, 42, *98*

Prinias, Crete, 26; Temple plan of, *26*, *27*

Propylaea, Athens, 31–32, *53*, *60*, *61*, *62*, *63*; Eleusis, 47

Propylon of Sanctuary of Athena Polias, Pergamum, 38, *72*

Prytaneion, Athens, 33, *48*

Public markets, *see* Agora

Pylos, 20, *19*; Palace at, *17*

Red-figured vase, *50*

Religious building, 37; *see also* Sanctuaries, Temples

Rhamnous, Temple of Nemesis, 29

Roman Market, Athens, 40, 41, *92*

Roman architecture, influenced by Greek, 47–48

Round Building, Tiryns, 18, *13*

Samos, 21, 25, 27, 32; first Heraeum, 21, *23*; second Heraeum, 25, 32, *24*; third Heraeum, 27, *36*; fourth Heraeum, 27, 38

Sanctuaries, 24, 35, 44–45

Sanctuary of Pandrosos, Athens, 31; of Artemis of Brauron, Athens, 32, *53*, *64*; Delos, *93*; of Apollo, Delphi, 44, *108*; of Asklepios, Kos, 44, *105*; of Zeus, Olympia, 46, *106* *107*; of Athena Polias, Pergamum, *72*; of Zeus, Priene, 44, *89*

Sardis, 38, Temple of Cybele, *68b*

Sculpture, use of, 26, 30, 31, 43, *31; see also* Frieze

Selinus, 30, *34e–h, 35*

Shrine of Demeter, Eleusis, 34, *47*

Sminthe, Temple of Apollo, 38, *69b*

Sophocles, 23

Stair Hall, Knossos, 17

Stoa, 24, 32–33, 39–41, 45; at Assos, 40, *88*; of Attalos, Athens, 40, *84, 85, 86, 87*; Middle Stoa, Athens, 40, 45, 65, *110*; "Commercial Agora," Athens, 40; of Zeus, Athens, 32–33, *66*; South Stoa, Corinth, 39, *82, 83*; of the Italians, Delos, 40–41, *93*; at Miletus, 40, *90, 91*; at Priene, 40, *89*

Sunion, Temple of Poseidon, 29

Syracuse, Temple of Zeus, 32, *34a*

Tegea, 39; Temple of Athena, *74, 78*

Telesterion, Eleusis, 33–34, *47*

Temples, 9, 11, 18, 21, 22, 24, 25–35, 37; *see also* Cella; Naos; Sanctuaries; Treasuries; Erechtheum

Temples, individual: of Aphaia, Aegina, 29, *51, 52a*; Early, at Aegina, 29, *40*; Concord, Akragas, 30; of Zeus, Akragas, *34b*; of Athene (Parthenon), Athens, 30–31, *53–56, 64*; of Athena (Old), Athens, 29; of Athena Nike, Athens, 32, *63*; of Athena Polias, Athens, 31, *35c*; of Butes, Athens, 31; of Hephaistos, Athens, 9, 11, 31, *2–5*; of Poseidon, Athens, 31; of Zeus Olympios, Athens, *68d*; of Apollo, Bassae, *52c*; of "Apollo," Corinth, 29, *35b, 38*; of Artemis, at Garitsa, Corfu, 25–26, 30, *31*; of Artemis, Ephesus, 25, *45, 46, 68a, 70*; of Artemis, Magnesia, *69c*; of Artemis Leukophryne, Magnesia, *71*; at Messa, 38; of Apollo, Didyma (Miletus), 38, *68c, 80, 81*; Naeandria, 26, *25*; of Hera, Olympia, *35a*; of Zeus, Olympia, 29, *52b*; "Basilica," Paestum, *34d, 42*; of Athena (Ceres), Paestum, 28, *34c, 39, 41*; of Poseidon, Paestum, 30, *52d*; of Athena Polias, Pergamum, 38, *72*; of Athena Polias, Priene, *69a*; at Prinias, *26, 27*; of Nemesis, Rhamnous, 29; of Hera, Samos, 21, 23, 24, 36, 37; of Cybele, Sardis, 38, *68b*; Selinus; "A," "C," *34e*; "D," *34f*; "FS," *34g*; "GT," *34h*; of Apollo, Sminthe, 38, *69b*; of Poseidon, Sunion, 29; of Zeus, Syracuse, *34a*; of Athena, Tegea, 39, *74, 78*; of Apollo, Thermon, 25, *21*

Theaters, 33, 41, 42–43

Theaters, individual: Athens, 42; Delos, 42, *99*; Delphi, 42, *99*; Epidaurus, 42, *97*; Megalopolis, 41; Pergamum, 42, *99*; Priene, 42, *98*

Thermon, 21–22, 25, 26; Megaron B, 21, *21*; Temple of Apollo, 25, *21*

Thersilion, Megalopolis, 41

Thessaly, neolithic building at, *11*

Tholos, Athens, 34, *65*; Delphi, 39, *73*; Epidaurus, 39, *75, 79*

Thrace, 14

Thucydides, 23

Tiryns, 18, 20, *13*; Mycenaean Palace, *14*; Round Building, 18, *13*

Tombs, 15, 18, 19, *16*; of Cecrops, 31; *see also* Chamber tombs

Treasury, of the Siphnians, Delphi, 29, *43, 44*; of Atreus, Mycenae, 19, *16*; of Gela, Olympia, *33b*

Tri-Columnar Hall, Knossos, 17, *7*

Trojan War, 21

Tsangli, Thessaly, *11*

Vase, 21; archaic Athenian, *32*; Geometric, *20*; Octopus, *18*; Portland, *111*; Red-figured, *50*

Vaulting, 37

Wars, Athens against Sparta (Peloponnesian) 24, 36; Persian, 24; Trojan, 21

SOURCES OF ILLUSTRATIONS

American School of Classical Studies, Athens: 2, 4, 12, 17, 48, 66, 82, 83, 84, 87, 110

Antikensammlungen, Munich: 50, 51

Annuario della Regia Scuola Archeologica di Atene, I (Instituto Italiano d'Arte Grafiche, 1914): 26, 27

Courtesy of the Archaeological Expedition of the University of Cincinnati; watercolor by Piet de Jong: 19

Athenische Mitteilungen LV (Deutsches Archäologisches Institut): 36; LVIII: 23, 24

Bagenal, Hope, *The Rationale of the Classic*: 22

Edgar Bissantz, Carmel, Calif.: 3, 85, 86

Courtesy of the British Museum: 46

Courtesy of the Brooklyn Museum (Department of Ancient Art): 18

Buschor, E., *Die Tondächer der Akropolis* II (Berlin, 1933): 33A

Clarke, J., Bacon, F. & Koldewey, R., *Investigations at Assos* (Cambridge, Mass., 1902–21): 88

Deutsches Archäologisches Institut, Athens: 20, 72, 75, 77

Dinsmoor, W. B., *Architecture of Ancient Greece* (London: B. T. Batsford, 1953): 7, 34, 35, 52, 68, 69, 70, 94, 102

Durm, J., *Handbuch der Architektur* (Leipzig, 1910): 105

École Française d'Athens: 74

Evans, Sir A. J., *The Palace of Minos at Knossos* II (London, 1928): 6, 9

Fouilles de Delphes II, 4 (1925): 73

Alison Frantz, Athens: 5, 8, 10, 15, 41, 54, 56, 58, 59

Furtwängler, A., *Aegina...* (Munich, 1906): 40

Hege, Walter, Karlsruhe: 60, 61, 63

Jahrbuch des Deutschen Archäologischen Instituts XLIX (1934): 100

Journal of Hellenic Studies LXII (1942): 91, 109

Kjellberg, L. and Boelhau, J., *Larisa am Hermos*, (Stockholm and Berlin, 1940): 49

Knackfus, H., *Baubeschreibung* (Berlin, 1941): 81

Krauss, F., *Die Tempel von Paestum* I (Berlin, 1959): 39

Lullies, R., *Greek Sculpture* (New York, 1957): 31

Foto Marburg, Marburg/Lahn: 16, 37, 43, 62, 79, 97

Matz, F., *Geschichte der Griechischen Kunst* I (Frankfurt, 1950): 29, 30

Georges de Miré, Paris: 44

Courtesy of the Metropolitan Museum of Art, Fletcher Fund: 32

Müller, Kurt, *Tiryns* III (Deutsches Archäologisches Institut, 1921–38): 13, 14

Nomlas-Fotos, Athens: 55

Pausanias, *Description of Greece*, tr. by W. H. S. Jones (New York, 1918–35): 106, 108

Phoenix, XIV (1960): 53, 64

Richter, G. M. A., *Archaic Greek Art* (Oxford, 1949): 1

Robertson, D. S., *Greek and Roman Architecture* (Cambridge, England, 1945): 21, 25, 35C, 71, 95, 104

Courtesy of the Royal Institute of British Architects: 70

Courtesy of the Royal Ontario Museum (University of Toronto): 53, 64

Shazmann, Po, *Kos* I (Berlin, 1932): 107

Schede, M., *Ruinen von Priene* (Berlin, 1934): 98

Schleif, H., *Olympische Forschungen* I (Berlin, 1945): 33b

Robert L. Scranton, Chicago: 28, 93

Courtesy of Staatliche Museen zu Berlin: 101

Stuart and Revett, *Antiquities of Athens* (London, 1762): 76

Travlos, J. E., Athens: 4, 17, 48; *Ephemeris Archaiologike* (Hellenike Archaiologike Hetairia, Athens, 1950–51): 47; *Poleodomike Exelexis ton Athenon* (Athens, 1960): 65, 67, 92

University Prints, Cambridge, Mass.: 45
Hirmer Verlag, Munich: 42, 78, 111
Verlag Gebr. Mann, Berlin: 80
Wace, A. J. B. and Thompson, M. S., *Prehistoric Thessaly* (Cambridge, England, 1912): 11
Wagner, H., Heidelberg: 57, 99
Weinberg, Saul, University of Missouri: 38
Wiegand, Theodor, *Priene...* (Berlin, 1904): 89, 103
Wycherley, R. E., *How the Greeks Built Cities* (London, 1949): 90, 96